The Road Less Travelled

Thriving through the long wait for a child.
One woman's story.

By Anita Benson

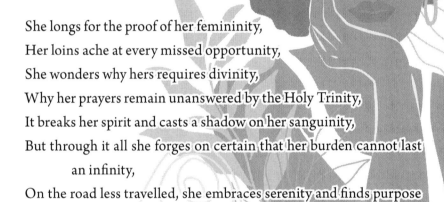

She longs for the proof of her femininity,
Her loins ache at every missed opportunity,
She wonders why hers requires divinity,
Why her prayers remain unanswered by the Holy Trinity,
It breaks her spirit and casts a shadow on her sanguinity,
But through it all she forges on certain that her burden cannot last
      an infinity,
On the road less travelled, she embraces serenity and finds purpose
      in mundanity.

Table of Contents

Introduction

Ave sat on the toilet trying hard to ignore the cramps. She knew what they meant but this time she was going to have 'big faith'.

"I am a joyful mother of children"

"I am a fruitful vine"

"I am pregnant"

She had been sitting there for half an hour and was running late for work. She didn't want to wipe herself, but the tissue was her litmus test on mornings like these.

She held her breath and wiped and there it was, the faint pink stains that heralded the torrent of red soon to come like a train, always on time.

She tried to comfort herself that maybe this was implantation bleed, but she knew the drill, she had been here 108 times before.

She got up with a heavy sigh. Her eyes glistening with unshed tears.

"According to a report by the World Health Organization, one in every four couples in developing countries have been found to be affected by infertility."

Some get pregnant after some months/years of trying, others never do. A one in four prevalence means that it's something we cannot ignore. We all know someone or a lot of people who have struggled or are currently struggling with it. Conception miracles are still one of the most celebrated, yet society doesn't do enough to alleviate the burden of the couples struggling with fertility. Fertility treatments are steep, health insurance rarely covers them and to make matters worse society low key stigmatizes these couples while turning a blind eye to their struggles. It is different from other sicknesses because embedded in tradition is the belief that an infertile woman has done something to deserve it- perhaps some wrong choices in her youth or *pissed off* some powers that be. Religion sometimes adds to this burden by giving conditions that must be met before the blessing of conception is bestowed. Conditions that are often never ending.

It is the road less travelled not only because one in four couples find themselves on this bumpy road but because this road is very lonely, often dark, and rife with dangers, heart ache and despair. No woman prays to be isolated, ridiculed, mocked, or continually disappointed month after month by an empty womb. No woman hopes to get to a point where her maternal instincts become a longing unfulfilled. Waiting to fill your cradle can be the most difficult wait you ever encounter in your entire life. Few couples even survive the grueling years and those who do come out changed, often for the worse but it doesn't have to be this way. Joel Osteen says, "though we are often more interested in the destination, God is interested in the journey. He is working on us along the way and walking with us through it all. When we understand that waiting doesn't mean that nothing is happening, doesn't mean God has forgotten about us and it's all a part of the process, then we can stay in faith knowing that at the right time God will get us to where we are supposed to be."

This is my story. The story of one woman who crossed all her t's and dotted all her I's and didn't for one minute think she would ever find herself on the road less travelled, but she did and amidst the tears and the lows, she learned to fight, to thrive and to protect that which she had already been blessed with. This is not an easy book to read, society is often uncomfortable discussing the plight of the waiting woman simply because most are guilty of an insensitive word or action or perhaps just a general lack of empathy. Even those sympathetic to her plight cannot fully understand because no one, not the doctors or even family can, unless they have walked in her shoes. I tell this story from the dual point of view of a waiting and hopeful young wife who has been married for nine years and counting and the experienced medical doctor who has been in practice for over a decade. I have played the role of patient and doctor countless times and I better than most, understand the two sides of the divide.

I hope this book gives you the waiting woman, strength to carry on, faith to stand strong and a strong will to thrive despite your circumstances. I hope this book gives you the new wife a sense of awareness and enlightenment, so you know how and when to act. I hope this book gives you the casual onlooker, some insight into the plight of your sisters, relatives, friends, colleagues, patients, and neighbors so you understand what these women are going through and perhaps offer a little empathy, speak with some sensitivity, offering a kind word and some support instead of the thoughtlessness that the status quo permits.

Thrive while waiting, God wouldn't have it any other way!

CHAPTER ONE

Why Me?

This was not supposed to happen to me. No bible-believing, covenant-keeping, tongue-talking, virtuous sister got married thinking she would not be able to have kids. My medical history was stellar, my sexual history practically non-existent till I met my husband, my mom had 4 kids, and my period was regular and normal. This was not supposed to happen to me!

But alas, month after month, I waited for God to show the world what I already knew, that I was His favorite daughter. I waited for His validation, for the validation of my marriage, for the fruit of all the lovemaking I legally indulged in and all I got was my menstrual period like clockwork. At first, I consoled myself that at least that meant nothing could be wrong, perhaps God wanted to give me some extra-special kids. The ones worth waiting for, customized and heaven's best. Still, I waited and soon I grew weary.

I bargained with God on many days, especially the days leading up to a menstrual period when I could feel the tell-tale signs in my womb. I reminded Him that I had done everything by the books. I had quelled my sexual urges as best as I could in university and given the man I married the gift of my virginity, a virginity that had been tied to a covenant and sealed with a chastity ring courtesy my 'Reverend' mom. I reminded Him that it had been hard walking away from my body's needs and wants and that I'd gotten bruised and escaped tons of near misses for His glory, so this was not supposed to happen to me. It didn't stop the devil trying to add on doubt by reminding me of the near misses. The days I had perhaps gone farther than I should, almost crossing the line, way past the acceptable good girl limit.

He wasn't going to let me forget. It didn't matter if I had prevailed at the end and stood my ground. The devil is not called the accuser of the brethren without reason.

I learned in my bargaining days with God that our righteousness could so easily become filthy rags before Him, soon I turned to grace. It was by grace that I had been saved. Grace had given me the right to be called His daughter and to stand in His presence unaccused. I was entitled to His promises regarding children not because I had obeyed one commandment in His book passably but because He loved me unconditionally and had given me all the rights and privileges that came with my status as beloved. This, however, did not stop my bargaining. When a problem lasts long enough for it to redefine your thinking and become part of your identity you come up with your own reasons for the why. Maybe like the differently abled man at the pool of Bethesda your 'why' is that the water is too deep and there is no one to carry you in and before you get there, someone else goes in before you. Whatever your argument may be, it becomes powerful enough to fight your conviction at the moment when you require your strongest faith. For me, my reason for the why was religious but misguided and altogether damning. 'It's God's will'. It became my mantra; it became the thing I said after I shed the pre-period tears and the thing I said when I failed to understand why God would answer all my other prayers but ignore this one that touched me the deepest.

Through it all, the 'why me' question hung in the air, friends and family who got married long after me, eagerly welcomed new life, effortlessly I might add. My husband soon began to suspect my mid-monthly sexual fervor. He felt the toll of each unmissed period and began to see each sexual act as a failure to attain the desired end point which a long time ago had stopped being a good orgasm. He had never gotten anyone pregnant and struggled with feelings of self-doubt within himself. There was a lot of pent-up emotions and built-up pressure, but we tried our very best not to sacrifice our marriage on the altar of infertility. We tried to celebrate the moments and make the days as fun as we could. We learned to support each other in new and meaningful ways and protect each other from the harshness of unwarranted human opinions and accusations. We certainly didn't deserve this. I remember during our marriage counselling they had asked us what God's purpose for marriage was and being the church girl I am, I had said with much aplomb- 'to be fruitful and multiply' and surprisingly the Reverend had said I was wrong. It was one of the reasons but not the main purpose for marriage. When he talked about companionship, two becoming one and cleaving as God's main purpose for marriage I remember shrugging it off because basically marriage was a package deal and we got to tick 'all of the above' in the options box. I thought of that conversation over and over as I settled into the wait. Some friends would complain about their marriages and tell me how lucky I was that my husband and I had been able to forge a strong relationship and become such good friends and attuned lovers. They said having a kid too early ruined that and sometimes they felt like strangers with each other. I would smile but not buy into the theory because despite the reasons they gave, I still wanted their picture perfect, children in the picture- life.

At some point I struggled with the thought that my inability to get pregnant was spiritual. It was a thought that one or two well-meaning sisters of God had put into my head when our medical tests kept coming back clean. One of them had expressly said unexplained infertility was spiritual and that modern medicine could not explain everything hence the caveat. It didn't take me long to adopt this new thought as there was already a vacuum created by the prolonged silence from my Father upstairs concerning this issue. The devil of course had already created the fear props and settings for this epic movie and for a while I allowed his version of reality be mine. The first house my husband and I had lived in after marriage had the landlord and an older, childless couple as our neighbors. We had heard that the landlord was quite fetish, one of the neighbors had reported seeing him bring some men in red with a tortoise and chickens to make sacrifices in the compound a while before we moved in. His family didn't miss church, so we ignored the rumors for a while. The house also had some unexplained unrest with the dogs in the compound beginning to bark as soon as the clock struck 3am every single day. What was making them bark? I would wake up in a slight panic and immediately start aggressive prayers till my peace returned and I went back to sleep. Again, I didn't think much of this because I had been warned when I moved to Benin city after marriage that unexplained, spiritual things happened all the time here and had come prepared for spiritual warfare. Then one night, some days after my always-on-time period was delightfully late, I dreamed that a man had struggled with me all night, repeatedly kicking me in the belly and when I woke up that morning there was blood on the sheets. I was very perturbed. This was definitely an attack! Then there was the day a bat had flown into my neighbor's house while I was there and everyone else was laughing and unmoved while I shrieked and ran to the kitchen to take cover. There always seemed to be a reason to go on my knees and battle in the spirit in this new city. This all culminated into a showdown between my landlord and me totally out of the blue. The Landlord had thrown a Christmas party and amid the festivities had asked to speak to me. My husband had gone with me, but he had pointedly told my husband that he wanted to speak to the person who had 'power' in the house. My husband was upset and clearly confused but gave us a little space though he stayed within earshot. The Landlord said to me in a challenging voice, "You think you have power; I have tested you repeatedly and you think you are strong. I see you wherever you are in your house, I see what you do. But you are not stronger than I am" and then he added in a sarcastic voice, "Don't worry you will have children." When my husband heard the last statement, he squeezed the wine glass he was holding in his hand so tightly that it broke. I was for the most part speechless. I had suspected the man of being evil but never thought he would confront me in broad daylight talking about powers! That night, we called our parents and our pastors. They prayed, we prayed but the advice was the same- find a new home and move out as soon as possible. We eventually moved out stealthily to our 'house of peace' and I put some distance between everyone who lived in my old neighborhood and myself. Hubby had decided he wanted to be more than a regular Christian and had worked on his personal relationship with God and even taken up a leadership position in church. No longer would any contrary power cast him aside for being weak!

When brethren talked about spiritual delays of conception, I would passionately recount the tale above and end it with a 'keep praying for us' and 'the devil cannot win' phrases. For a while, it answered my whys and I felt that surely since I had prayed hard enough and overcame the attack, conception would happen any day soon. What I didn't realize was that this new belief gave the devil the upper hand. It conveniently made me forget the bible verse that says, once has He spoken, twice have I heard, that all power belongs to God (Psalm 62:11). As long as I was still low-key living in fear, I had not accepted that the battle was already over or won. It reflected that I wasn't totally convinced that all power belonged to God. I had to take the final stand. I prayed aloud one day that if my old landlord ever attacked me or my family again- physically or spiritually or even set his eyes on us, his obituary would be announced. When I finished that prayer, I felt like a load had been lifted and my peace returned. I never did set my eyes on him again and it has been 8 years. He obviously got the memo. God is the final authority and He had promised that I could have children so no contrary word could out talk His. His word said, 'Don't worry about anything; instead, pray about everything. Tell God what you need and thank him for all he has done' (Philippians 4:6). Worrying was not permitted to be part of the agenda though I occasionally gave in. I often reminded myself that I had a covenant with God, and He always kept His promises. It wasn't out of place to think that this spiritual win would translate into a pregnancy victory but there I was month after month, praying for the fruit of the womb, eagerly shouting "Yes Lord" and "Amen Father" to every prophecy and prayer about conception. Waiting, hoping, researching, struggling to hold on to faith simply because I just didn't think life was being fair to me at all. Basically, back to my status quo but a little different from when I started the journey. I still did not have any answers to my whys, but I had learned on this journey to let go of my sense of entitlement and pride, we are saved by grace through faith and not by ourselves, it is the gift of God, not of works, lest any (wo) man should boast (Ephesians 2:8-9). I had learned to not give in to spiritual oppression even while I waited. My fertility was solely in God's hands and the devil did not have a seat at the table. It took a while to understand and let go of the 'perhaps it's God's will' state of mind and I'll admit I still struggle with that sometimes, but I needed to see God for who He really was, a loving Father. I didn't need a covenant to deserve God's indescribable love and unmerited favor, nothing could ever separate me from His love (Romans 8:37-39). Yet marrying this revelation with my daily denial and endless waiting was hard and, on many days, I still struggled with accepting that God really loved me. To me He was like a lover who was acting out of character, I didn't want to doubt His love so instead I kept making excuses for Him so that His love could be justified in my eyes. I would tell myself that perhaps if I had a baby in 2013, I would have died or had complications so instead He made me wait a little or some other plausible excuse. Trusting when you don't have all the details is the highest form of love. It took me years to begin to even fathom the idea that I might never understand why He made me wait this long but that He loved me and because of that love I had to trust that He had the very best of reasons for the wait.

Your story may have begun a little differently, perhaps there is something you felt you did in your past that may be responsible for your childlessness. Perhaps your reproductive organs are beaten down by an abortion or catching an STD or some other baggage from your past choices. Sometimes the devil can paint a convincing picture of worthlessness. When the Holy Spirit convicts you of sin, He will always direct you toward a specific action that you can take (John 3:19-21) but most times all it takes is coming to Him on your knees to genuinely repent. God loves you too much to hold a past mistake over your head. He says I hid my face from you for a moment in a surge of anger, but I will have compassion on you with my everlasting gracious love (Isaiah 54:8). Learn to distinguish God's voice. God will never condemn you or make you feel bad. Our feelings of worthlessness usually stem from self-judgment or the devil's negativity. We are sinners, saved by grace and it's wrong of you to take responsibility for your childlessness when you cannot do a simple thing like turning one hair on your head grey. If we wrongly take responsibility for our infertility, it is because we do not understand that God is the giver of life. There are men and women who did whatever it was you carry guilt for and still have children, that same grace abounds for you. Jesus made sure of that! So, turn your guilt over to God so you can bask in His grace for His word says, 'He is made strong in our weaknesses' (2 Corinthians 12:9). His word also says, but if it is by grace, it is no longer based on works, otherwise grace is no longer grace (Romans 11:6). The devil will in these moments of waiting seek for ways to fill you with doubt, guilt, and self-loathing. His ultimate plan is to make you feel so defeated that you feel unworthy of God's love and unable to pray. I know because I have been here in this dark place several times.

Infertility deeply affected the way I viewed myself. I wondered if perhaps I wouldn't make a good mother or maybe I was paying for a previous sin or had been cursed by some agent of darkness or some bad karma. I even began to imagine that perhaps I had some yet to be diagnosed genetic anomaly. How could God deliberately withhold this blessing from me? A woman in church had jeeringly asked me how I could stay so happy and fashion conscious when I was unable to give my husband a child. 'Christian women' continually told me how lucky I was to have a man that would stay with me through my childlessness. Childlessness can have a profound emotional impact on your self-image and personal well-being. I once walked out of church mid-service in tears because I couldn't understand how this loving God could pass me through this excruciating wait. I had never been a patient person and now it was certain that one of my lessons was to learn to be patient and to let go and let God. He says, be still, and know that I am God (Psalm 46:10). Being still is perhaps the most difficult thing to do when you wait for something especially if an end date has not been provided. It's so easy to be plagued by negative thoughts when waiting to conceive. You wonder if God will ever answer your prayers, you wonder if your husband will be tempted to have children outside your home, you wonder if your in-laws will stop being so understanding and start giving you trouble, you wonder if your marriage will survive childlessness, you wonder if your missed period is going to be another 'late period', you wonder if the expensive fertility treatments that you can barely afford will work, you wonder if you will carry your pregnancy to term this time. A lot of wondering! So many women are plagued by these negative thoughts, and they influence their actions, words, attitude, and countenance but it doesn't have to be so. The more you think these thoughts, the more you are likely to live these thoughts so instead think about things that are beautiful, kind, nurturing and wholesome. Think about testimonies you have heard of women who have had beautiful children despite their initial delay or doctor's diagnosis. Think lovely thoughts about your marriage, husband, and in-laws. Think intentionally, think like your thoughts were magic thoughts that shaped your destiny because truly your thoughts determine your tomorrow, and we want a beautiful future! His words say, 'whatsoever things are true, honest, just, pure, lovely and of good report...think on these things' (Philippians 4:8) and as a man thinketh in his heart, so is he (Proverbs 23:7). Counter every negative thought you have with a positive fact! A testimony of God's goodness to you or someone you know usually helps give the much-needed positivity to chase away negative thoughts. Don't stress about the why, live in the now and know that a victory a day makes the wait a little easier to bear. Remember that it is God that gives power to conceive. He made a virgin pregnant (Mary), He made menopausal women pregnant (Sarah and Elizabeth), He made a woman with unexplained infertility pregnant with twins (Rebecca), He made a scorned woman pregnant and took away her reproach (Hannah), and He made the beloved wife a joyful mother (Rachel). God has the power to help you conceive regardless of your age, medical report, past or circumstances. His word says, 'casting the whole of your care [all your anxieties, all your worries, all your concerns, once and for all] on Him, for He cares for you affectionately and cares about you watchfully' (1 Peter 5:7). He is all powerful and He has promised that none will be barren so forget your preconceived whys, *why don't you trust Him today?*

Prayer

Dear Heavenly Father, you knew me before you formed me in my mother's womb. All the days of my life are numbered, there's nothing that has or will ever happen to me that you are not aware of. Nothing happens to me without your permission. Thank you for taking ownership of me, thank you for your faithfulness and unconditional love. Thank you for seeing me as you see Jesus.

Lord I ask that you strengthen me during this period of waiting, that you surround me with your love and increase my joy. That you keep my home in perfect peace even as I wait for your promises to be made manifest in my life. Thank you, Lord, for loving me immeasurably, thank you for the plan you have for me for I know in this matter the end will far surpass my expectations. Thank you, God, for being the God of the impossible, the all-powerful God and the God who is personally on my case. Thank you for my victory. Help me to see my life just as you see it and to find rest in you in Jesus' name I have prayed. Amen

Action points

1. Draw a table in your personal journal or notebook with three columns. Column 1: Why you think you deserve children. Column 2: Why you think you do not deserve children: Column 3: What God says about you having children in His word. Now confess your feelings about worthlessness and guilt and other negativity expressed in column 2 to God. Let him grant you peace and where indicated, forgiveness for any past mistakes. Let him fill you with His love and peace so that you can be still, like a cool breeze while He sorts out your life in a way that surpasses your expectations.

2. For the next 10 days, write daily affirmations on a sticky note to counteract any feelings of worthlessness or despair and post them on your mirror and fridge. Back them up with scriptures. Here are a few examples:
   - I'm beautiful (Psalm 139:14 I praise you because I am fearfully and wonderfully made)
   - I'm worthy (Romans 8:1-2 Therefore there is now no condemnation for those who are in Christ Jesus. For the law of the Spirit of life in Christ Jesus has set you free from the law of sin and of death.)
   - I deserve to be a mother (Psalm 113:9 He settles the childless woman in her home as a happy mother of children. Praise the LORD).

3. Start a Gratitude Journal. Every day write down everything God did for you that day even so-called little things like helping you get to work on time. Gratitude changes your attitude.

4. Write out 5 reasons why it may have been medically impossible for Sarah to conceive and then take a moment to ponder on why her son was named Isaac which means laughter!

CHAPTER TWO

The Struggle

Every day was a struggle simply because the world had its own ideas about why I was unable to conceive and consciously or unconsciously made them known to me. I had worked in health care settings for years and I knew what the doctors thought and what the world thought caused an inability to conceive. Most were shrouded in shame and stigma. Stigma for past sexual indiscretions leading up to infertility or the shame of having a body that didn't work the way it was supposed to. Bearing children was an essential part of our society and it was often an anomaly to see a childless woman thrive regardless of her situation. The world felt the need to stop her and remind her that she couldn't, every time she thought she could. I ticked a solid 'no' to all the uncomfortable questions the Gynecologist asked about my sexual history, had my period every month without fail and without complications from the day after my 12th birthday and didn't have any medical illness or genetic disorders connected to infertility. I was a medical doctor and had devoted my life to helping people. I had cared for so many children both medically and financially that if there was a cup of good deeds in heaven for this sort of thing, mine was surely running over. I had even wanted to be a pediatrician at some point, before my path led to me to some other medical specialty. I looked 'fertile'- well according to a couple of my Igbo suitors back in the day, who said they knew these things, so it hurt perhaps a little more to be forcefully put in a box that I did not think was the right specification for me.

Every other day, a young girl would come to do a scan at my workplace, and I'd see her new life, a life she didn't want because it had come with the package deal of unprotected sex when all she craved was a little fun. I'd cringe, my smile plastered on my face, trying to counsel the young woman while she talked carelessly about having an abortion. All the while asking God why? Why was my faith being mocked? Why were seemingly less-deserving women getting that which I desperately wanted, that which I certainly deserved? All I got was silence...sometimes some peace after a good cry. There were two incidences I never forgot. A young girl was rushed in with signs of appendicitis, she required an urgent scan. She was accompanied by three young men who claimed to be her neighbors. As soon as I put my probe on her abdomen, I saw the baby. She hadn't even known she was pregnant, had not bothered to find out why her period was late/irregular and wasn't even sure who the father was. The pain she was feeling was early labor and after the initial shock she was taken back to the referring hospital for proper care. There was such a buzz at work that day about her cryptic pregnancy and a couple of remarks made within ear shot about how girls were wasting children while some married women desperately wanted children. I wept that day. Why did I have to witness this seemingly unwanted miracle? Another young girl had come for a scan with her boyfriend just prior to going for an abortion and I had seen not one baby but three. She was expecting triplets and she wanted to be rid of them. I had counselled her, asked to speak with her alone and counselled her again. She hadn't even stayed to pick up her report. Her mind was made up. I had printed a pic of the triplets for her, and that pic stayed on my desk for weeks, I would look at the beautiful embryos and wonder how life could be so unfair. My job description at the time entailed counselling women on infertility issues and other pregnancy related issues and many a woman cried in my office about her inability to conceive or made flippant remarks about her over ability to conceive and need for contraception or a termination of pregnancy. All through I had to keep my demeanor professional, personal issues aside. The struggle was real!

I went from being a social butterfly to an antisocial recluse. I dreaded the question that always followed social introductions. "Mrs. B, how are the children?" One friend instructed me to always say 'fine', but it only led to more uncomfortable questions, so I stuck with my truth. 'None-yet". But the nosy ones pressed on, giving loose-lipped prayers as the look in their eyes revealed their conclusion about my situation. 'She must have blocked her tubes with all those abortions...these city girls, whatever it is, it's HER fault.' I wanted to be left alone. I stopped going to church on Mother's Day and Children's Day. I was selfish about protecting my happiness. I'd skip a baby dedication or party if it was going to steal my joy and plunge me into the agonizing darkness that came with my deepest longing. Ashamedly, sometimes I was angry with God. I was also angry with all the prophets who gave me an expiry date to my problem and yet apparently forgot about it and me when that date passed without any respite for me. I prayed more than I had ever prayed in my life, I gave more than I had ever given in my life-sowed seeds of faith, gave gifts of thanksgiving, gave my tithe faithfully. I confessed scriptures, I bought baby clothes but every month the day before the period, I'd feel the sensation that heralded yet another period. I'd cry unto God, beg, bargain, plead, confess scriptures, pray but the period would come, red and defiant, sometimes with menstrual cramps that worsened my sorrow. Year in and year out, this was my cycle of pain and disappointment.

My body began to play tricks on me and occasionally, my period would delay for a day or two, once even for a week. I would have symptoms, but I didn't know which symptoms were real and which symptoms were due to PMS (premenstrual symptoms), I just hoped that they were pregnancy symptoms but soon rather than later the period would come. There was a woman who came into my consulting room one day, she hadn't seen her period for almost five months, had all the pregnancy signs and symptoms and a protruding abdomen but all pregnancy tests and ultrasound scans were negative. One doctor had even referred her to a psychiatrist. As I carefully scanned her abdomen and saw nothing, I felt her pain. She was convinced she was pregnant; her body was behaving pregnant; she could feel the baby move so why wasn't anyone seeing it? I had read about phantom pregnancy (pseudo pregnancy) a long while ago and tried to gently educate her on how the brain could interpret the intense desire for a baby as signals for pregnancy which could trigger the surge of hormones like estrogen and prolactin leading to actual pregnancy symptoms. I made her see it wasn't her fault and she wasn't crazy and then encouraged her. I wasn't completely sure if she was totally convinced but she seemed much better and more accepting than when she walked into my office.

Ovulation days were filled with hope. I counted my days carefully then checked them on my phone apps to make sure I had all days covered and then I would buy the ovulation predict strips for good measure. I was ovulating but pregnancy wasn't happening and then at work, more than once I would inform a woman who hadn't ovulated in months or who had irregular menstrual cycles that I could see her beautiful fetus in her womb. It made no sense to me. Medicine had honestly failed me. The womb watchers at work were another bone of contention. If I added on a little weight, they would exclaim loudly that perhaps I was pregnant. They commented about my diet, my habits, my choices, relating all to my inability to conceive. All said in a supposedly good-natured way and accompanied by loose lipped prayers so that I would not see this emotional abuse and invasion of my privacy as an offense. A friend asked me repeatedly to shut them down, but I craved peace and harmony and rather chose to ignore them, claiming I was blocking out the negativity. I wasn't, I was internalizing it. Absorbing it like harmful radiation.

Every woman single or married who had ever been pregnant had some advice for me. Many were unorthodox and appalling to my doctor brain.

They wanted me to get my womb massaged, that perhaps it was too hot. They wanted me to take a lot of different herbs. They told me about women who could make me get pregnant even though I would continue to see my period every month till delivery, but I had to deliver the baby in a hospital of their choosing. (I later learned this was a nefarious practice where they induced a fake pregnancy with drugs and then gave the woman a paid for, usually stolen baby). They told me about prophets who would take me up to the mountain to pray and I would return pregnant. They told me about rivers I could bathe in that would remove any infertility problems. One even advised me to sleep with my ex incase my husband was the problem. I was asked to lose weight or gain weight depending on what school of thought the one giving the advice belonged to. I was given prescriptions and recipes, concoctions, and therapies. The advice was always unwarranted but nothing I could do or say stopped these people. Some even forgot I was an experienced medical practitioner and would diagnose me by merely looking at my face, claiming that I resembled a friend of theirs who had blocked tubes and then ask me to do so and so or go to doctor so and so who was great at handling such a problem. More often than not, the doctor turned out to be a traditional healer in a white coat! These people had success stories for every remedy offered, some of them personal stories but I ensured I did vast research and asked the hard questions before adopting any of their methods. Those that my spirit was against, I did not even consider. A lot of them probably felt offended when I did not take their advice and it was disheartening sometimes to hear a person say I deserved what I was going through since I was so stubborn, but I stood my ground. A lot of the women who have had children through dubious means are quietly bearing the consequences. I wanted blessings that added no sorrow.

As a doctor, one of my many struggles was having to become a 'patient' sometimes in the hands of practitioners who were less experienced or empathetic than I was. My husband had noticed a while after marriage that

I had milk coming out of my nipples and we had done a serum prolactin test which had come out elevated. Since I was ovulating every month, the doctor felt it wasn't the cause of my infertility but nevertheless prescribed medication for it. It took some months for my prolactin to normalize, and my husband and I were introduced firsthand into the world of extortion that many patients looking to conceive are introduced to by get-rich-quick doctors, when a family doctor made us pay ninety thousand naira for a brand of medication for hyperprolactinemia, only for my husband to find the exact same brand at a high brow pharmacy for ten thousand naira. Infertility is good business for many unscrupulous doctors because they know you will do anything and pay anything to have a child. My prolactin levels normalized but still no baby. I remember the first time I had to do a HSG (Hysterosalpingogram). It was a test to show if my fallopian tubes were blocked or patent and if my womb cavity was alright and it was notorious for being very painful. Prior to my fertility testing, I had never been admitted in a hospital, never had drip (intravenous infusion or drugs) and never had surgery, now I look at my new list of 'nevers' and smile. The test was painful but came out normal which was a relief. The other hormonal tests all came back normal and so did my husband's sperm analysis and scrotal scan which made doctors for many years dismiss us and ask us to 'keep waiting' or consider 'assisted conception' if we were tired of waiting. Of course, we didn't think we needed an IVF (in vitro fertilization) since we were 'normal' but the idea of being normal was also the greatest source of our frustration. If we were normal, why didn't we have children? At least if there was an obvious problem, we would have an obvious prayer request for healing and the doctors would have an obvious disorder to treat.

I depended heavily on emotional eating and as a result my weight fluctuated a lot. Food helped me cope. A chocolate bar and a bowl of ice cream usually was enough to fix my sad countenance and give me back my happy albeit temporarily. Hubby had stopped regular social drinking because he had been educated about the adverse effects of alcohol as well as cigarette smoking and recreational drugs on male fertility and would indulge in my sweet treats occasionally. Much as I loved the euphoria of a sugar rush, I hated the weight I was adding on, and I was on a constant diet-binge cycle. I tried so many fad diets but always turned to calorie overloads on my cheat days. Food kept me calm, food helped me cope, food made me happy. Food didn't judge me or disappoint me, and it was a close friend who gave me creature comforts whenever I required them. But alas, I needed to be slim and sexy because the world had sold me the idea that a barren wife was easily replaced so I wanted to be the irreplaceable wife. The hot, successful, great cook and home maker, sexy, amazing in bed, supportive, virtuous wife that made him the talk of the town and the envy of his childbearing friends. I did not want to be replaced. I reminded myself that Sarah was old and barren, but Abraham had to lie that she was his sister to keep from being victimized when the king wanted her. I imagined how beautiful and together she must have been even at her age besides society hadn't given me permission to be anything else.' New sentences: I imagined how beautiful and together she must have been even at her age. I felt pressured to be like her because society hadn't given me permission to be anything else. Acceptable weight gain, stretch marks, frumpiness and falling breasts were peddled in society as a consequence of childbearing, since I didn't have children what on earth was my excuse? I soon learned that striving to be perfect pissed off another set of society's demographics who felt I was overcompensating, and they felt the need to rub their children in my face to prove to me and to themselves that the one achievement I failed to attain was indeed the most important.

Spiritually I was struggling too. I was accused indirectly of not praying enough or not having enough faith even by those closest to me and I wondered how they felt they were able to correctly deduce the goings on in my secret place to my Heavenly Father. I was gifted books by so many amazing authors, and I read and reread these books. I made confessions about supernatural conception, and I soon joined the bandwagon of those mandatorily invited to miracle services by the world because they had concluded that I needed a miracle. I attended some special services in different bible believing churches, attended vigils, got prayed on and anointed, baptized, and fasted more times than I didn't. My husband and I picked baby names for our unborn children, we wrote them down and prayed over them often. We bought baby things and had them anointed in church. We were given bottles of anointing oil and anointed handkerchiefs from far and near and sowed seeds and made countless vows all in the hope that God would finally take notice. I always left every pastor I bumped into with the parting word that he should pray for me, and he always ended the prayer with 'it's settled' but was it really? Why did we still feel like we were hanging on the precipice just waiting for another period to shatter our hopes?

The struggle has torn many couples apart and broken the spirit and faith of many. A man who struggled with infertility told my husband that he had gone 'outside' to test his manhood on another woman who claimed she was now pregnant just to be sure the problem wasn't his. A woman I knew whose husband had been diagnosed with zero sperm count (azoospermia) had allegedly gone 'outside' to sleep with someone else to save face for the family. There were times I didn't even want to step foot in a church. Times I felt so forlorn and sad that I was ready to give up, perhaps even consider walking out of my marriage so that my husband would be free of me and my woes. He always assured me that he didn't marry me for children and that he loved and treasured what we had regardless of what we didn't have. I would struggle every time I saw my husband play so happily with other people's kids. The children loved him, and he loved them, and it made me unworthy that I was robbing him of fatherhood. I didn't know for sure if it was my fault, but society always laid blame on the woman, and I had unconsciously accepted my blame. I put up a wall around myself, not wanting to be too familiar with other people's kids so my heart wouldn't ache, not wanting to be too close to anyone so they wouldn't ask me the difficult questions. I relied much too heavily on my husband for friendship and emotional support. I never wanted to go out or hang out and if I did, I was always in a hurry to leave unless I was the one organizing and, in that case, playing perfect hostess. He knew how social and outgoing I could be and perhaps felt a little sad that life had made me lean more heavily towards the introverted part of my personality.

People struggle in many ways with infertility. Infertility has led to addiction, extra marital affairs, aloofness, over ambition and conflict. It's important that during this wait you find a way to block out negativity and stay grounded. To find pleasures in simple things and give yourself a break as often as you can. One thing that helped our struggle for a while was finding another couple who were like us- young, fun, in love, trying to conceive and on the same spiritual wavelength. We organized many couple getaways and get-togethers and helped each other through some of our personal struggles. Another thing that helped our struggle was family support. Find those family members who are like a breath of fresh air and would protect your peace and happiness over anything, if you don't have any family like that, find a friend who would stick closer than a brother. The Lord always gives us some respite in our daily struggles and in those times when you feel the most overwhelmed, He is there right by you, holding you close. Don't let this struggle break you. Fight for your marriage, fight for your peace of mind and sanity, fight for your happiness. Leave the things you can't control (like childbearing) in God's hands but refuse to allow them destroy life as you know it. Do not let the struggle stop you from living your best life. Do not make hasty decisions for quick fixes that will negatively affect your health, marriage, or peace of mind. Wait well! The bible says that after you have suffered a little while, the God of all grace [Who imparts all blessing and favor], Who has called you to His [own] eternal glory in Christ Jesus, will Himself complete and make you what you ought to be, establish and ground you securely, and strengthen, and settle you (1 Peter 5:10).

One remedy for my struggle that I constantly engaged in was the power of praise. God inhabits the praises of His people (Psalm 22:3). Praise is a very powerful weapon, the only tool that Paul and Silas needed to break out of prison (Acts 16: 25-26) and the only weapon that the Israelites needed to bring down the walls of Jericho. Your ability to praise God with your whole heart is one of the first things the devil tries to steal from you when waiting to conceive. Micah, wife of King David was the only woman in the Bible to have been cursed with inability to have children for the rest of her life because she mocked her husband while He was praising God. A lot of us may have done worse but thank God for the power of the blood of Jesus, our atonement for sins. That blood that was shed wiped your slate clean and it releases you from any curse, mistake, or past transgressions. So, you don't have to worry or fear, regardless of the doctor's diagnosis or the strong man's decree, when praises go up, the children come down! If not praising God caused Micah to have a closed womb, surely praising God as David did will open any womb and bring forth our promised children (2 Samuel 6: 16- 23). During my wait, I learned about the power of praise, and I surrounded myself with praise and worship songs, on the days I was alone, driving to work on my daily commute, I'd let myself go, singing at the top of my voice and connecting with my God through song. The praises filled the gap my repetitive prayers couldn't fill. They expressed my gratitude and absolute trust in my Maker and by the time I was arriving at work, I was super charged and excited knowing that beyond doubt my children were on the way!

Poem by Teresa of Avila

Let nothing trouble you,

Let nothing scare you,

All is fleeting,

God alone is unchanging,

Patience,

Everything obtains.

Who possesses God nothing wants.

God alone suffices.

Not one of all the Lord's good promises to Israel failed; everyone was fulfilled (Joshua 21:45).

Prayer

Dear Lord, you see my daily struggles, you more than anyone knows my pain, my tears, and my sorrow. Please grant me peace, show me a way of escape. Lead me beside still waters and green pastures and restore my soul. Help me not to bring Ishmael into my life while waiting for Isaac. Help me to be patient. Help me not to depart from your presence in a quest for a quick fix. Help me not to break faith with you in this hour for I know that your promises are sure and your arms a safe place from the storm. Please fill my mouth with praises and bring me to a place of rest as I joyfully wait with certainty for my children in Jesus' name. Amen. Thank you, Lord.

Action points

1. Write an honest list of your personal struggles with infertility and prayerfully write a counter list of how to tackle these struggles in a way that leaves you peaceful, happy, and content.

2. Get two awesome praise and worship CDs/DVDs/playlists to play on repeat every chance you get.

CHAPTER THREE

You vs. the World

The people you let into your life while you wait can make or break you. Not everyone should have access to you, not everyone should be allowed into your inner circle. You are like a little plant in a big field, some visitors could do you more harm than good. Humans have the potential to speak words of life or words of death into your life, every informal interaction sows seeds of encouragement or seeds of despair the longer you entertain it. You cannot entirely block out your species, but you can choose who you grant prolonged audience to (outside formal business interactions) and those who you allow yourself to have an emotional reaction to, whose words you allow yourself to internalize. They will in no doubt influence your outlook during the period of waiting.

I learned early on that people could be quite insensitive to my plight. No matter how wise, spiritual, or seemingly loving a person was, if they had never walked in your shoes, they were prone to an insensitive remark every once in a while. The sad part was they were often oblivious to the effects of their words on your person and on your mood, like a dance partner unaware that he had stepped on your toes. I learned to forgive these remarks but also to distance myself from people who hurt me with their words so that I could stay happy. The distance gave me closure and eradicated any bitter root that may have sprung up because of those insensitive words. I guarded my happiness and peace of mind jealously and trod cautiously in social circles because it was hard to know from whence the next missile would be thrown. Family for obvious reasons always cut the deepest. I was quite close to a relative who was much younger than I was and when she gave birth soon after marriage, I went to visit her along with a friend. I was about to leave when she warned me 'jokingly' that the family would call a family meeting over my head if I was continually unable to give my husband a child. It was the only time I had ever heard negativity from family regarding my situation and I was shocked and upset, although I hid it well enough. I kept thinking about it over and over and it didn't help that my friend who accompanied me was also deeply offended by the remark. I internalized the feelings and soon had myself worked up about my days as his wife being numbered. I eventually told my husband about the incidence, he and his family showed me how protective they were of me by the way they sprang into action to right the wrong and reassure me of their collective love and support. His family believed that children were a blessing bestowed by God at His own time and had never made me feel bad about waiting. The lady called to apologize and said she had expected me to speak up if her joke offended me. We parted ways, not because I thought she was a bad person but because at this point in my life, I needed to protect my heart from the bearers of flippant words. A lot of people forget that they have to be careful of their choice of words when dealing with you and their insensitivity greatly adds to the burden.

Even in church, I noticed the exuberance of members to always usher my husband and I to the altar when prayers were being said for fertility and their difficulty with understanding why I would sometimes choose to not leave my seat. Sometimes their eyes showed their disapproval. Some thought it was pride, but I had an understanding with God. He knew I wanted children, I had asked him more than a million times and gone out to the altar more times than I could count so since my request had been unequivocally submitted upstairs pending review, I would stay put! Sometimes I would be asked to sow a sacrificial seed for my fertility, a seed that would 'move' God to act. In retrospect, I can tell you that these seeds were sown out of sentiments. God does not need your money to bless you with children. Spirit led giving from a cheerful heart will always be more pleasing to God than sentimental giving for performance sake.

There was also the world's reaction to my finances in the wake of having a small family of two. A member of my church once chastised me in quite an entitled manner for not sowing more into her children's lives as in her opinion that was a guaranteed way for God to answer my prayers. Some colleagues at work would beg me to lend or give them money and say 'after all what was I using my money for, I had no kids'. It irked me that people would say such things to me when they needed a favor from me, and it opened my eyes to what others facing somewhat different challenges were going through especially those who were believing God for a spouse. I tried to be more sensitive in my dealings with them because with all the stress people pass through while waiting, they do not need the added stress of dealing with poor attitudes. It's quite amazing that the world castigates the people whose problems are worn as obvious labels without realizing the two most important things- 1. Everyone has problems and 2. Those with the greatest problems are usually the ones whose problems are concealed and not obvious to the casual onlooker. Image is really everything and that's probably the reason why women waiting for a child, or a partner are generally under the most pressure especially from other women regardless of their other victories and accomplishments. Don't let the world define how you should spend your money or live your life or what you should aspire for especially not in the wake of your 'problem'. Enjoy the blessings you have been given freely without prejudice or care while you look up to God for the fulfilment of the promise. The world's opinion is irrelevant.

A man I respected a lot had asked me why I didn't have kids yet and then had gone on to say I had better give my husband kids before my mother-in-law brought in a girl from the village and then proceeded to go on and describe rather lasciviously and to my utmost horror how attractive and curvy village women were with their round hips, hairy legs, unshaven armpits and ever welcoming arms; fresh, natural, and submissive not like the city women everywhere. I felt bad for his wife, he had certainly given me an unwanted glimpse into his secret fantasies, and I wanted no part of his ideals. A few men offered their reproductive organs to me to help me with my 'husband's' perceived problem, one even asked me to leave my husband that he would marry me and give me children. Some married men would talk inappropriately about how 'tight' I must be and how my husband must be 'enjoying' since childbearing hadn't widened my plumbing or altered my body yet and I would be torn between my pain at being viewed as an 'anomaly' and feeling genuinely insulted about their leery comments. I realized at this point that how I portrayed my marriage to the world was very important as well as how I portrayed myself. The world already viewed me as broken and perhaps desperate and certain people would not miss an opportunity to take advantage of me or sow seeds of discord in my heart.

Sometimes I would meet women who were far younger than I was, who called me by name and yet insisted on me calling them 'mama A' or 'mama B' per tradition, because I needed to accord them the respect childbearing bestowed on them. These same women would turn around later to beg me for a favor of some sort usually financial help or free medical treatment and I realized that they probably didn't remember the hurt they had meted out to me when they reminded me of my place in society since society made it okay to say such things, to speak 'their truth' regardless of who it hurt. On one of my birthdays, I had gotten a cake and stayed home, and a couple of friends had come over and as they ate cake the conversation had moved on to their children and stayed there. They all had kids and for the next couple of hours they had talked about their children and everything pertaining to them while I fidgeted uncomfortably and said 'I can imagine' from time to time. All my subtle nudges to change the conversation fell on deaf ears. It was my birthday hangout, they were supposedly close friends, they were sitting in my house eating my cake and yet without even trying too much they were ruining my day for me and passing me through agonizing reminders of my pain. Eventually it was time to leave. Later that night, one of the women called me to apologize for their insensitivity. The others remained oblivious. I tried not to take offense because I had been in this situation countless times though never in my own home and not with friends who should know better. I learned to accept the fact that when women of a certain age came together, they only discussed their children, other women, and other people's marriages or compared assets. Thankfully, I was able to meet other women later in life, who changed this perception and preferably talked about their careers, passions, hobbies, making the world a better place and other wholesome, neutral topics despite having families. I learned not to be too quick to accept the norm, if I was having trouble fitting in then my best bet would be to change the crowd I was rolling with. I also learned the value of 'excusing myself' from an uncomfortable situation or conversation. The next time I was with a bunch of women discussing their children I quietly exited the scene, and I was better for it. Preserving my happiness and peace of mind not only made me a wholesome person but when I was happy, my husband was happy. My mood invariably rubbed off on him and it was my duty to ensure I didn't bring garbage home.

Then there were those who assumed they knew exactly what was wrong with me and how to fix it. One day out of the blues, a woman had called me to go see a doctor who was very helpful with blocked tubes. I was chagrined and immediately let her know my tubes were fine. There was someone else who only called me when her children were ill and needed free medical advice. She never once called to ask how I was doing or offer support for my situation but during intimate gatherings always seemed eager to shift the focus of discussions from me and my achievements to her kids and how wonderful children were in general. After a while, I began to doubt that it was mere coincidence. She invited me to speak to some mothers virtually about their children's health and I tried to play along for a while but realized the pressure of being on a moms' group in my current situation was more than I could handle, and I opted out of the group. It took a few years before we could give our relationship another shot. I realized that even though friends and family may not be the cause of your problem, not all of them are capable of making your waiting time less painful and sometimes for reasons unknown, they may derive some small pleasure from your discomfort. Just because they are close to you does not mean you have to entertain words that will break you instead of building you up.

One former hair stylist of mine was another person who felt she knew exactly what was wrong with me. She had diagnosed me with 'elephant pregnancy'. She said elephants waited about five years before they could conceive, and some women had it too and would sometimes wait up to nine or ten years before and between pregnancies. She went on to say she thought the problem was with my husband because no man would continually be so nice to a childless woman if he didn't have his own secrets. She was on her second marriage, the first broke down due to childlessness and needless to say, I found a new hairdresser. I also realized that I needed to be careful about letting certain people who had gone through what I was currently going through free access into my life. It's not everyone who is travelling on the same road with you that is going to your destination. I have met women who tried to impose their beliefs, disappointments, and fears on me in the name of offering me wise counsel and takeaway lessons from their own life experiences. I once met a woman who had been waiting for the fruit of the womb for almost twenty years and she tried to make me understand that the sooner I accepted the fact that my husband would have a child outside the less painful it would be when it happened. Another woman would share stories about how every procedure she had ever done had failed and how she had tried everything, and God had not shown up in her case. Even though she was a lovely woman, and our conversations were deep, I found out that her stories made me more afraid, less trusting in God's ability to answer my prayers and filled me with despair. I eventually had to give her some space even though I missed the friendship. One other woman was convinced that a particular person was responsible for her infertility and spent most of her days in spiritual combat with this diabolical human and the more her prayers remained unanswered the more she lost faith in God's power and dreaded more each day the dark powers working against her till she began to believe as evidenced by her conversation that the only way out would be to beg the woman responsible or fight dark power with darker power.

Even though I deeply respect every waiting woman's struggle and the experiences that have molded them into what they are now, I have come to realize that I must be deliberate about my choice of friends amongst women who are waiting, or I may end up being molded by other people's experiences. While making this deliberate choice about whom I let stay in my life, I resolved never to judge a woman who was on this journey with me since I had not lived her life or endured her unique struggles. Every woman's wait is different, her pain unlike yours. If you are strong in an aspect of the wait do not despise another who struggles in her journey. If you are always strong and joyful, do not look down on the woman whose wait is riddled with complaints and sorrow. Everyone has a different threshold for pain and God deals with each of us differently. If you have it a little easier in some respects for example, having a supportive husband or in-laws who do not make your life a living hell, do not trivialize the pain of another woman who doesn't have it as good. Even on the collective journey there are avenues for one woman to be insensitive to another while they wait so be mindful of this and if a woman's energy clashes with yours or her stories get you down instead of lifting you up, be careful how you part ways, do not add to her grief or make her feel inferior. It would not please God. I gravitated towards women of faith who didn't stop believing that God would turn their situation around. I gravitated towards women who were thriving, happy and successful while they waited. Women who had strong, happy marriages despite the wait and women who had information on the newest technological advances, and *it* places where fertility was concerned. Most importantly, I gravitated towards women both waiting and 'arrived' who left me happy, hopeful, encouraged and invigorated after every conversation and interaction. It wasn't that these women didn't have 'off days' or times when they felt down, despondent or discouraged but what made them so amazing was that they didn't wallow. They accepted the good days and the bad days but didn't let the bad days keep them static. They kept moving, kept thriving and kept living their best life. They were light and they lit others up, they never ever snuffed out another's light and they never allowed their darkness to consume them!

There were times that people used my apparent strength as an excuse to justify inappropriate behavior. My seeming acceptance and niceness towards all unsavory comments seemed a come-hither for more. Some people would tell me about one woman or another that God had blessed with a child or pregnancy and ask when God would answer me. I started calling these women 'pregnancy announcers' as the only time they called or came to visit was when, yet another female had conceived. I believed that one day these same women would announce my pregnancy. I think they justified their messenger status by thinking the news 'encouraged me' rather than realizing that the constant announcements only made me feel truly forgotten on Heaven's waiting list. Many times, I questioned their motives. They seemed to derive more pleasure than necessary from their announcements. Nevertheless, every time I heard news, I genuinely rejoiced for these newly pregnant women because it had always been my firm belief that when God blesses someone close to you it means He is in your neighborhood- so prepare your heart to receive.

As the years passed and more and more friends failed to make the cut due to their persistent insensitivity, God brought new people into my life. Amazing friends who carried me in their arms with a love born of God. I had friends who never brought up my issues unless I did and were always patient listeners with soothing words who did not presume they had all the answers or even pretended to understand what I was going through. They were there for me in any way I needed them to be, and I counted them as sure blessings from the Lord. I had friends that would call to check up on me even though the phone had to ring repeatedly on several days before I picked. They did not take offense that I had developed an aversion to phone calls and were not swayed by my cheery voice or work- related excuses but listened closer for any strain in my voice and always provided some salve for my wounds. They were the friends who instead of judging my binge eating and fluctuating weight encouraged me to go exercising with them where we spent long hours talking and laughing. Those moments were always so therapeutic. There were also friends who would wake me up to pray at night, pray with me and for me, encourage me with messages and scriptures, fast with me and generally provide much needed spiritual support. There were friends who never let me say one self-depreciating word about myself. If I called myself fat, they would remind me how beautiful I was and if I felt bad about my inability to have a child, they would remind me about all the awesome things I had accomplished and firmly reassure me that I would bear children. These friends were always in my corner and during my IVF journeys stayed close, praying for me, advising me, crying with me when I felt overwhelmed, offering me their strength when I was weak and respecting my silence and distance when I needed to be alone. Finally, there were friends who I could share my deepest fears and darkest thoughts with, and they helped me stay accountable and stay strong and together we crossed crazy hurdles. I am grateful for these friends.

I learned from this journey that I had absolute control of who I allowed in my life. Sometimes I felt guilty when I removed the access pass someone had to my life but the more I did it, the more I realized how much peace came with it and the shorter I waited before doing it again when the need arose. Over the years, some friends became family while some family were demoted to mere acquaintances. I was selfish about my mental health and gave little or no room for negativity to take root or yield fruits. I realized that truly the world was full of amazing people, and it was up to me to pitch my camp with them. I didn't end friendships with a 'fight', no! We simply went our separate ways like Abraham and Lot did- usually my decision but surprisingly none of the friends I gave 'space' ever confronted me about my sudden distance. It was like they expected and accepted it. It made it easier for the sanguine part of my personality to stick to my resolve. I decided that I would rather have three real friends than scores of fake ones, the numbers did not measure the quality of these relationships not when I was in this sensitive situation that I hadn't chosen for myself.

Prayer

Father Lord please bring meaningful friends into my life. Friends who will stick closer than a sister. Sisters who are born for adversity and who will walk with me on this journey. Father any frenemy currently in my life, please give me eyes of understanding to decipher who they are and wisdom to walk away from the friendship. Please protect my heart from the insensitivity of the people around me and help me never to be bitter about it in Jesus' name.

Action Point

Who are your real friends? Write a list. Don't force anyone to make that list and don't make excuses for the behavior of anyone who should have made that list. Invest more into the friendships that made the list.

CHAPTER FOUR
When God Says No

I had been married for five years when I decided to do an IVF (in vitro fertilization). I had been thinking about it off and on for a couple of years and it took a little while to get my husband fully on board. After he agreed, I checked online and asked around for the best centers for the procedure. A friend messaged me out of the blue prompting me to do an IVF, she also had been waiting and had just done one and encouraged me to meet up with her at the fertility center she used as she was about to do a blood pregnancy test, two weeks post-embryo transfer. I talked with her doctor about the process in general and the cost. I liked the place where she had done her IVF because it was faith-based but it was well above my budget. My cousin met up with me afterwards and encouraged me to keep looking. I spoke to a couple of medical colleagues and was directed to a doctor who had been doing his residency program when I was a house officer. He gave me a good discount and seemed altogether friendly. I didn't mind the long commute to his hospital in Festac town. I just wanted results. God provided the IVF payment supernaturally. We didn't plan towards it or save towards it. God just caused the money to be available when we needed it without borrowing or stress.

I was doing my residency subspecialty training and was a bit worried about getting some time off work for the IVF, but God granted me divine favor and my trainers were very understanding and gave me the time I needed off work. The first thing that struck me about the clinic were the baby pics lining the walls of the reception. So many babies! I looked at them wistfully, dreaming of a time when my babies would also grace those walls as another success story, privacy momentarily aside. The second thing that struck me about the hospital were the number of women in the waiting room. It was almost like a general hospital. All these women waiting for a miracle after years of battling with infertility, each person's story different. There were young women, middle aged women even elderly women and there was a solemnness in the air that I couldn't shake off.

I liked the fact that my doctor seemed very enthusiastic about my case. He said my tests were essentially normal and I was young and that he couldn't understand why I hadn't been able to conceive naturally and hopefully the IVF would be the answer. He was a cheerful fella who would walk into the hospital reception and say 'Namaste' with a slight bow as a form of greeting to all his patients. He wanted me to do a hysteroscopy (a procedure to look into the womb) and a womb scratch because scratching the womb lining created grooves that made it easier for the embryo to implant. The hysteroscopy turned out to be the most painful and traumatic procedure I have ever had till date. I wasn't given an epidural, just some injection pain killers and something to dilate my cervix and how I cried and screamed. My mother was downstairs in the reception and said she could hear me wailing and it broke her heart. I felt like God had abandoned me. I cried for the Holy Spirit's help during the procedure, but the pain progressed. I was weary from all the crying and sleepy perhaps from the meds, but the pain seemed everlasting. Finally, it was over and there was nothing of note to report from looking in my womb which had now been successfully scratched. The doctor said my womb and lining looked beautiful and healthy on scan and my husband's sperm was good enough to fertilize my eggs. We wouldn't be needing donor eggs or sperm. I was teased for being a doctor who couldn't endure pain but for the most part the staff were quite sympathetic of my plight.

I started treatment on the 11th of September 2017. I was shown by the nurse how to inject myself and placed on some daily injections, oral medications, and vaginal pessaries. I had never injected myself before and I had an intense fear of needles but still I trusted myself more than anyone else to get the job done with the least pain. Every time my alarm went off for my shots my heart would beat a little faster. I told myself I had to keep enduring because it was for a good cause, and I would be carrying my babies soon. God kept me through the process, 21 days flew by so fast. Estrogen increases the body's ability to form life threatening clots. I took over 80 tablets of this hormone and God kept my blood clot-free far beyond the abilities of the protective 75mg of Vasoprin I had been prescribed. I never had an injection abscess and the only side effect I had which was tenderness and cord like feel of the vein they used to give me intravenous infusion in my wrist (superficial thrombophlebitis) resolved in answer to my prayers. I had been warned that I may gain lots of weight, break out with pimples, have unwanted hair on my face or chest and that there was a risk of ovarian hyper-stimulation syndrome which was very serious and potentially life threatening. I had only three follicles which apparently was very few. The doctor seemed confused that I hadn't produced more but decided to go on with the procedure. Egg retrieval was scheduled for the 4th of October. I was given two options-intravenous painkillers or general anesthesia. I had never been put under even though many of my patients had been, on my watch. I was torn between my phobia for surgically induced pain and my phobia for medically induced sleep. There were about ten women scheduled for egg retrieval that day and the woman who went in before me picked the general anesthesia option. She returned about an hour later in a wheelchair, saliva drooling, unable to move unaided and even though her eyes were open she had a vacant expression on her face. The next patient who had opted for intravenous pain relief walked in not long after, cheerful and vibrant. I made up my mind on the spot. No general anesthesia for me! Of course, the first patient was good as new after sleeping it off for a couple more hours but I just didn't feel comfortable being that detached from reality plus I only had three follicles so the doctor had said my procedure wouldn't take more than a few minutes. I sucked it up, went in and got my eggs retrieved while I was awake. During the procedure, I prayed and spoke in tongues and confessed scriptures and rebuked fear the way I had learned to in the Supernatural childbirth book by Jackie Mize and just when the pain was reaching its peak, it was all over.

The next step was the wait for a phone call from the hospital telling me how many healthy embryos had formed from my eggs and my husband's sperm. The phone call came two days later. I was informed that two of my three eggs had fertilized to become embryos and only one had matured. I was to come in the next day to have the embryo transferred. I got in and I could tell from the look on the doctor's face that the odds were against a one embryo, day 3 transfer. My faith was tuned to maximum, and I let him know that God only needed one. He said he had been waiting for the embryo to die but it didn't, he blessed the embryo and said he genuinely hoped my prayers would be answered. The procedure was over before it begun, I was informed an embryo was put in although I wasn't shown the embryo before it was put in. It was a procedure of 'trust'. I don't even remember the discomfort associated with it. For the next two weeks, I prayed, fasted, waited on the Lord, sang praises, worshipped continuously, and confessed scriptures. I went online to read testimonies of women who had only one embryo put in and now had a child or even had multiples because the embryo split in the womb. Travis Greene's song 'Made a way' was on repeat on my phone and in my heart. The doctor called on day 12 of the 2 weeks wait to see if per chance I was still having pregnancy symptoms as opposed to a period and God did not let me have a bad report to give. He sent me a text on the morning of my appointment to ask if my period had come and again, God did not let me have a bad report to give. I was indeed hopeful. On October 23rd, 2017, I went to the hospital with my husband for the blood pregnancy confirmation test. The doctor informed us that he had already gotten some successes that day and hoped we would add to the number. I learned later that IVF centers ensured you knew about the successes of their other patients so that any failure in your case would not be attributed to them in any way.

He took my blood for the qualitative and quantitative pregnancy tests and left to conduct them. I was anxious and went to the car to wait, asking my husband to be the bearer of the news. While in the car, I prayed and sang praises and confessed God's word. My husband returned about 45 minutes later and one look at his face told me what I dreaded had become my reality. He tried to calm me down. Told me the test had come out negative and that the doctor had said we should have done egg batching. I went from being sad to being upset after hearing his concluding words. Why hadn't we been offered all our options during the cycle? Why was this the first time I was hearing about egg batching? Wasn't a longer process with a better outcome more desirable than this failed procedure which suddenly felt rushed? My husband tried to calm me down as best as he could, given the fact that he was also upset. I managed to send a text message to the doctor thanking him for his efforts despite the outcome. He did not reply, and I did not hear from him again for almost a year. Neither was there any provision made for counselling or follow up by the hospital. I wasn't surprised though, I had heard that many IVF centers treated the patients with failed procedures like lepers, distancing themselves until they felt the patients were sufficiently ready to pay a premium for a new cycle. I got home and did a urine home pregnancy test as a sign of faith. It turned up negative.

My anger increased by the day. I was angry with my husband because he got over it too fast or so it seemed, and I accused him of not being emotionally invested enough in it. Men have their own way of expressing grief. His expression of grief was different from mine, and I needed to respect our differences and know he felt as badly as I did even if he was 'manning' it up. I was angry with Travis Greene. I couldn't stand his song after that. It irked me, it felt like a lie. God hadn't made a way. I eventually got over it but still have mixed feelings every time I hear it, a sort of love-hate relationship with the song. Ashamedly, I was also angry with God. He had made me waste money, go through horrendously painful procedures, have new life put in my womb then have it snuffed out. Had not answered all my prayers or hearkened to my spiritual confessions. The procedure had even tallied with my church's annual fast, and I had joined them when I could and yet nothing. I didn't understand it, couldn't accept it. I almost left the church. I couldn't wrap my head around an unconditional love that permitted such pain. My fear of Him was the only reason I didn't turn my back on the faith. I was a mess! I didn't even have my friends to lean on because I hadn't really carried them along. The procedure had been painful and private and rife with uncertainties and on any given day during the cycle, I had not had the presence of mind to discuss what I was going through with anyone. One of my friends felt bad about this and I hoped one day she would understand the emotional rollercoaster that IVF was. I hadn't wanted her to pity me or hear me cry neither had I wanted her to see me so weak, uncertain, and broken but that seemed to be my present state of mind every time she called, and I kept our phone calls brief. She was also waiting but had rejected the option of an IVF and a part of me felt letting her in on my pain in real time would make my decision seem like the wrong one. A lot of prayers had been said, mostly personal and from my pastor and family though I hadn't carried my prayer circle along but what had become of all these prayers when my answer was a cold and resounding NO?! There was also the nagging issue of informing those who knew about the IVF including my work colleagues that this girl's God hadn't come through for her just yet. It was as painful as the actual failed procedure emotionally.

I knew I needed to get my emotional and spiritual balance back. I started by reactivating my gratitude journal and writing out all the testimonies I had during the cycle. Testimony number one- God had used this IVF to grant me the opportunity to stay with my parents for 6 weeks, something I hadn't done since I got married in 2012 and it truly was a time of refreshing. No testimony was too small at this point. Testimony number 2- God had strengthened my husband and I through the abstinence period required for the IVF and kept us united and faithful to each other- it was the longest time we had ever been without sex. At this point I was prepared to thank God for oxygen. The more I wrote the little testimonies, the more I got reminded of the bigger ones and soon I had a very long list of His mercies. I knew I was broken and only gratitude and the recounting of God's faithfulness could restore my faith in His love for me and it worked! He also granted me an unexpected miracle- I call it the 'this too shall pass' miracle. In less time than I thought was possible, I had bounced back to my old self and the memories of my ordeal had all but faded away.

The bible says the Lord is close to the broken hearted (Psalm 34:18). Sometimes our hearts will be broken perhaps from a dismal diagnosis or a failed procedure. It may be hard to keep believing or even to understand that He could possibly still have your best interests at heart during the confusing ordeal. There's a poem called 'Footprints in the sand' and I want you to carefully read it and internalize it so that you may remember it when life hurts the most.

One night I dreamed a dream. I was walking along the beach with my Lord. Across the dark sky flashed scenes from my life. For each scene, I noticed two sets of footprints in the sand, one belonging to me and one to my Lord.

When the last scene of my life shot before me, I looked back at the footprints in the sand. There was only one set of footprints. I realized that this was at the lowest and saddest times of my life. This always bothered me, and I questioned the Lord about my dilemma.

"Lord, You told me when I decided to follow You, You would walk and talk with me all the way. But I'm aware that during the most troublesome times of my

life there is only one set of footprints. I just don't understand why, when I need You most, You leave me."

He whispered, "My precious child, I love you and will never leave you, never, ever, during your trials and testing. When you saw only one set of footprints, it was then that I carried you."

With time I remembered His promises, 'yea, thou shalt see thy children's children, and peace upon Israel (Psalm 128:6)'. The Bible is full of awesome promises, and it says God is not a man that he should lie; neither the son of man that he should repent: hath he said, and shall he not do it? Or hath he spoken, and shall he not make it good? (Numbers 23:19). That's why this amazing four-part blessing in Psalm 128:6 gave me so much comfort!

1. You will not be barren because barren women don't have children!

2. Your children will not be barren because they will give you grandchildren and they will live long enough to procreate!

3. You and your children will not die during childbirth so no worries about pregnancy or birth complications!

4. No worries about disasters that tear families apart because to see your children's children means you are not captive, your children weren't taken from you and you all live in peace and harmony, and they are not prodigal sons or daughters who have run away from home or shunned family!

Isn't this awesome? It's simply breathtaking. God breathed life into my situation by reminding me of these simple but profound and highly prophetic words that He had uttered!

Do not ever allow the devil for a second to make you feel abandoned or unloved by God. Do not let the thought that God is unconcerned with your pain or punishing you ever be entertained in your heart. You are precious to Him, and He will in no time give you joy in place of your sorrow and peace in place of your turmoil even if the joy and peace does not come in the way you expect or from the channel you hoped, it will surely come, and you will be alright again. He will never ever give us more than we can handle (1 Corinthians 1:13).

Not too long after my failed IVF I was informed that I had been shortlisted for the interview for a prestigious international fellowship. This was such a huge deal. I did the interview, and I got the fellowship which gave me more recognition, international travel, and influence than I had had in a long while. Joy always comes in the morning!

Prayer

Father help me to accept the things I cannot change and to never doubt your love or perfect plans for me even when I don't understand why you allowed some things to happen and help me not to give up on you because I know you would never give up on me. Thank you for honoring your word above your name and for your promises that are true. I find rest in your word because I know it will surely come to pass in Jesus' name. Amen

Action Plan

1. In your Gratitude journal, write out the little testimonies that sprung forth from the most difficult times in your fertility journey and how God showed His love and presence in your life.
2. Find meaningful baby names for your children and write them down and next time you think about your children, call them by name. Find other promises in the Bible that cannot be fulfilled if you don't have children, there are so many. Delight yourself in the fact that God honors His word above His name.

CHAPTER FIVE

The Gift

One evening early in the year 2019, my friend messaged me on Instagram. She was the friend who had taken me to see the doctor at the fertility clinic I had liked but which was beyond my budget just prior to doing my first IVF. She and her husband were about to be blessed with a beautiful baby girl after waiting for some years and as a sign of their gratitude to God wanted to pay for an IVF cycle for me at that highbrow fertility centre. My husband and I had not had any real plans for assisted conception for the year because we had some heavy financial commitments to take care of, nevertheless we were believing God for a miracle conception. I was overwhelmed by my friend's generosity. I had never actually been gifted anything of that magnitude and I wasn't quite sure how to thank her. I told my husband about it, and he was shocked and quite moved because like me, he came from a world where most people took from us rather than giving to us. He had only even heard of this friend of mine just once in the seven years that we had been married and it made the story even more astonishing that it wasn't one of the friends in my inner caucus who had made this kind offer.

When God wants to bless you, He brings His blessings through the most unlikely sources. I called my sister next, and the phone call was quite emotional. This was because just two months before she had asked about my plans to do a second cycle of IVF and I had told her about our financial challenges. Then, she had been of the strong opinion that I ask my closest friends and family for help, she was not in a position to help us financially at the time, but she was a firm believer in the power of a strong circle of support.

43

I had adamantly refused simply because I am one of those few people who never begs or borrows- call it a fear of rejection, a need for self- sufficiency or a principle of mandatorily cutting my coat according to my cloth. It was a principle I'd always lived by and coupled with my willingness to always offer help if it was in my capacity to do so, it probably would never have crossed the minds of most of my friends that I would need help. Most people assumed my husband and I were very well to do. I already imagined the plethora of excuses I'd get from my friends and ended up in tears when my sister got exasperated at my stubbornness. I was frustrated that God would even put me in such a situation that the talk of begging for help would be a serious topic for discussion. I had assured her (after the tears) that hubby and I were fine, and that God would sort us out somehow. I saw the tears in her eyes and the overflowing of her love for me and knew that if she had the means to give me the money, she would without a second thought.

I would tell myself on tough days that He would never let me be put to shame (Isaiah 54:4) and that before my back touched the ground, help would come. I would encourage myself with these bible verses about supernatural provision; Ask and it will be given to you; seek and you will find; knock and the door will be opened to you. For everyone who asks receives; the one who seeks finds; and to the one who knocks, the door will be opened (Matthew 7:7

I went in for my first appointment with high expectations. I wasn't a newbie, I had had an IVF before, and I knew the drill or so I thought. The first appointment broke my heart. The doctor asked for an ultrasound scan and some blood tests. I had done both several times before and could recite my past medical history like the multiplication tables we learned in school. I knew I had recently developed fibroids but previous reports had said they were 'intramural' meaning in the wall of the womb not in the cavity of the womb so we had always been reassured that they would not prevent conception and then I did the scan and I was told that there was a fibroid in

44

the part of my womb that the baby was supposed to implant on (the fundus). My last ultrasound scan had been in early 2018, more than a year before and this 'submucous' fibroid had not been present. The doctor told me I had to do an operation to remove the fibroid before they could proceed. Surgery??? I rejected it immediately. God's blessings made rich and added no sorrow, how on earth could they be leading me to surgery? Then the second bad news came rolling in. My AMH was low. The Anti-Mullerian hormone tests a woman's ovarian reserve and provides an estimate of the quantity of her remaining egg supply. For some reason my eggs were running out and the thought was devastating. I had been 'wasting' them monthly for 22 years with each monthly ovulation/menstruation cycle and now that I really needed them, unlike other women my age- my reserve was running low. I struggled to hold back tears. The doctor assured me that the quantity usually didn't affect the quality in younger women and that all it took for pregnancy was just one healthy egg, but the double bad news made seeing any silver lining that day nearly impossible. I had done several tests in the past, but no one had ever asked me to do an AMH, perhaps if they had, I could have been more proactive.

The thought of doing an actual surgery scared me so much. I decided I wasn't doing it and that God would just have to give me babies that implanted near the fundus. It took a friend of mine talking sense into my head for me to get a grip of my fear and decide to go ahead with the surgery. I know at this point you are wondering why a doctor would be so afraid of surgery. I had observed and performed quite a few successful ones but while practicing medicine, I got to hear of the unsuccessful ones, the mistakes, the complications, and the deaths that occurred. It made you only trust yourself and a handful of other medical professionals when your own life was on the line. I was informed that I would be getting an epidural and that the surgery would be laparoscopic meaning that I would not have a scar on my abdomen. I have a low threshold for pain and would scream whenever my blood was being taken so the thought of an injection in my back and someone cutting me on the inside filled me with dread. During the epidural, I had a 'panic attack' when the pain hit and had to be given some medication before they could complete the anaesthetic procedure. They allowed my husband into the operating theatre during the procedure and his soothing voice really calmed my nerves. I had a repeat of this harrowing procedure six weeks later so the doctors could have a look at my womb and give me a go ahead for the IVF. It also involved an epidural and unsurprisingly, I had another 'panic attack' after the needle was put in. I remember the surgeon telling me when he took out the fibroid that my womb would hold triplets and I had said a big amen before drifting off to sleep. One of the scriptures that kept me during this period was Proverbs 10:22- 'The blessings of the Lord, it maketh rich and He addeth no sorrow to it.' I believed that despite the setbacks, the only reason I was in that hospital in the first place was because God had blessed me through my friend and as a result no sorrow of pain, complications or death would mar the blessing. In the next couple of weeks, I heard of two women who died after this same 'routine' operation. One of them was my age and a medical doctor. I was reminded to never take the mercies of God for granted.

After the surgery, I was asked to commence medication for the assisted reproduction. I was also given the option of donor eggs as a backup if my eggs did not meet the expected quality or quantity. My last IVF had produced only three eggs while the average woman could produce ten or more eggs after stimulation. I wasn't a stranger to this aspect of medical counselling during IVF; indeed, I had counselled a few couples in my line of work prior to starting my residency program. I remember a couple who had male factor infertility. The husband had azoospermia (zero sperm count) and they had requested to speak to me about the use of donor sperm. He was considering asking his brother for sperm and while it was not in my place to dictate his final decision, it was my job to let him know the pros and cons of both sides of the divide. If he went with his brother, he would need to be sure the news didn't become family round table discussions amongst his relatives. We had had issues in the past where nosy family members took it upon themselves to inform the young child and even went as far as informing neighbours and teachers about the 'truth' behind the conception. There was also the possibility of his brother being unable to let go of his 'paternity' rights towards the child which may lead to future conflict. In favour of using his brother's sperm was the obvious fact that the child would be his blood relative and, in many ways, resemble his non-biological father. On the flip side, using a stranger's sperm could be a well-kept family secret between husband and wife because hospitals did not permit interaction between the couple and the donor to prevent future legal paternity issues. The stranger would also be screened for common diseases and hereditary conditions that could potentially affect the child. Usually, a stranger of the same ethnicity and physical appearance of the father was selected. Joseph the carpenter was not Jesus's biological father, but for all intents and purposes he was his father (Matthew 1:20, Matthew 13:55). The bible also said that a man and his wife would become one (Genesis 2:24) meaning that if this child had one set of chromosomes from either father or mother, the child belonged to them both. The couple asked for some time to think, and I gave them a week's appointment. They returned to thank me and inform me that they had decided to go with the donor sperm. The man further explained that the African culture was not yet welcoming to the idea of assisted conception much less donor sperm and that doing it 'quietly' would ward off unnecessary negative attention.

Asides the paternity or maternity of the child, using a donor is quite a delicate issue as it is easy for the parent who is not contributing biologically to feel left out or aloof about the whole process. This is usually preceded by private feelings of guilt and self-blame because they see themselves as the cause of the couple's long-term infertility or blame themselves for decisions made in the past which have led up to this moment. Women who use donor eggs take it a little easier than men for two reasons. First, they have the privilege of carrying the baby, so they get to bond with this child for 9 months before delivery and form the same attachments that biological mothers have. Secondly, they have some societal validation because the children they are carrying belongs to their husbands and they 'laboured' for the child. Typical well-wishers in the African setting are very concerned with finding resemblances between a new-born and his father. For a father who got a donor sperm, he may require constant emotional support, sensitivity, understanding and total inclusion in every process so that he develops a sense of ownership that far outweighs whatever negative feelings the devil may be tormenting him with. It's worthwhile to note that any man can be a father, but it takes a special kind of man to be a dad. There's a scripture the Holy Spirit laid in my heart about this situation (1 Corinthians 3:7), It says, 'It's not important who does the planting (whose sperm/egg) or who does the watering (whose womb). What is important is that God makes the seed grow. So, if you find yourself in this peculiar situation, stay thankful to the God who makes the seed grow and focus on being the best parents you both can be to your child.

The medication involved 7 injections and 25 tablets daily. I was a human infirmary! I tried not to dwell on the possible drug- drug interactions or adverse effects that could occur with my pill burden. I was traumatized every time I had to stick a needle into my stomach, thigh or buttocks and there were many times I didn't feel like the gift was a blessing, but I held on to the fact that this time would be different, that this present suffering was culminating into a great reward and that my endurance and persistence would be justly compensated. There was no going back, only forward. I realised that God had orchestrated this gift as a catalyst in my life. After my first IVF my husband had closed his mind to whatever gains IVF may provide and would not have been open to trying again even if we had the financial wherewithal. Without this gift, I would have continued to wonder at my unexplained infertility thinking it beyond the scope of modern medicine. Without this gift, I may have been less believing of the depth of human kindness or missed out on jumping on the 'pay it forward' wagon which I had unconsciously committed to. Without this gift, I would have continued to harbour an unnatural fear of some aspects of medical practice instead of trusting in the wisdom and skill God has bestowed upon my colleagues. The gift in many ways changed my outlook on life.

Often in your journey through infertility, God sends you a gift. A well written book that illuminates your mind about what you are going through, a new friend that brings a different type of aura and support, some financial assistance to help with the heavy burden, a prophecy or dream that renews your hope and invigorates your faith, some new medical information or a medical option that provides a window of opportunity, a change in scenery that allows for a fresh start or some other blessing tailor made for you and your situation. This gift always brings a change to our current mind-set so that we have a new perspective of the events that have shaped us. It is often the connecting bridge between our pain and our passion. The moment when we began to entertain the smallest possibility that God allowed us pass through this trial so that we in turn may be able to encourage some other woman who may be passing through similar struggles in future. It reminds us that amid our pain, God cares enough to call for a time out so we can catch our breath, reboot and re- strategize. Do not despise a gift no matter how small you think it is. There is a 'grace for rest' that is tied to it. Even a well-timed distraction from your current realities may be a gift. Something that makes you laugh unexpectedly or gives you something entirely different to think over. It's important to recognize and appreciate these gifts for what they do to your spirit and what they mean in your life. They are reminders that God cares and is invested deeply in our situation. They are reminders that He will not give us more than we can bear and always provides for us a means of respite.

God is never late! For you shall not go out with haste, nor go by flight; For the Lord will go before you, And the God of Israel will be your rear guard (Isaiah 52:12). We should never feel pressured to be hasty because He will be our rear guard. A rear guard watches your back! God himself is telling you "I got this!" so take your time. When it is time, He will put everything in place, from finances to time to expertise. Pray about the tests and procedures you are considering. Ask God to direct you to the best doctor, best laboratory, best adoption agency, best surrogate, best fertility options. Yes, God is available to help with the steps leading up to having a child. Ask Him every step of the way if this is His will for you. Get confirmation before you subject your body to all sorts of treatments. You don't need to hear a loud booming voice or a message for you through a great man of God, no you just need to hear Him speak to you through His word and have His peace take over your anxiety. If I do not feel peace within about a doctor or a procedure especially after praying, I am usually convinced that it is not God's will and God has proven again and again in my life that when I walk in His will for my life, I experience peace in my heart and in my situation, so I urge you not to be hasty. Pray about the next step and seek His peace. Remember the Lord Almighty is your rear guard! Trust God to do as He has promised and perform His word.

Prayer

Dear Heavenly Father, thank you for daily loading us with blessings and for your thoughts for us which are only of good and not evil to bring us to an expected end. Thank you because you make a way for us even when there seems to be no way. We ask for wisdom to understand your plans for our lives and grace to align ourselves with these plans. Your word says that we should commit our ways to you, and they will succeed. We commit every person we need to see and every test or procedure we need to undergo into your hands. We ask for wisdom, patience, and strength. We submit to your will with thanksgiving and in total obedience because we know that all things work together for the good of those who love you. We know that because you have promised that none will be barren, you have a divine plan to make us parents and right on time because you make all things beautiful in your time. In all things we will give you thanks, and we will keep worshipping you regardless of the outcome. Thank you for your grace that is sufficient for us. We bless you Father for always hearing us when we pray, in Jesus mighty name. Amen

Action Points

1. Have you done all the fertility tests required? (See a comprehensive list in Appendix 1)
2. What gift has God bestowed on you recently?
3. Every morning when you wake up, confess that you are a joyful mother of children, your children shall sit around your table and your quiver shall be full of them! You have what you say! The tongue is powerful.

CHAPTER SIX

The Process

My second IVF cycle started on the 7th of May 2019. Prior to that I had gone into the operating room twice to make sure my womb was clear of 'obstructions' and had another doctor's room procedure to double check. You would think that with all the cutting, injecting, and prodding my pain threshold would have reached a respectable level but that was far from the case. I cried and screamed and begged God to help me every time my body was subjected to these intrusions. I consoled myself that it was for a glorious end, and I was certain that God would not leave me to face this alone or ignore my bruised body and copious tears. I had called up one of my sisters and spiritual mentor to let her know that the cycle was starting, and she had sent me the word of the Lord about my situation and some sermons to boost my faith. She kept telling me 'I feel so much peace when I pray for you'. She had told me that once the main event (egg collection and embryo transfer) was about to start, she would set up a prayer circle for me so that a group of sisters would be praying for me around the clock all through till God confirmed His word. Her faith helped mine on so many difficult days. She sent me testimonies of women who had walked the path I was currently on and powerful, daily confessions to prayerfully say each day. God gives us the desires of our heart (Psalm 37:4) and deep within me I knew this one would be different.

The cycle commenced with me being placed on some injections. I had to inject myself every day and coupled with my fear of needles, each encounter was mentally harrowing. There were some days I had to take seven injections at a go- one in the morning and six at night. I had to inject my belly and my thigh and still had to go to the hospital periodically for other IV infusions. The needles were never ending. It got to a point that I was able to comfortable set an IV line for myself whenever the need arose. Something a lot of doctors cannot do on themselves. It gave me a deeper understanding and empathy of my patients. I became a patient, subject to the nuances and bureaucracy of the hospital where I was receiving treatment. On the day I had to commence the intramuscular injection in my thigh, I cried and cried on the dining table as I gazed upon the long needle that would soon be buried in my thigh. I had sent my husband an SOS message minutes before that I needed his strength and he had rushed home to meet his wife sobbing uncontrollably. I just didn't think I could do it anymore. I couldn't find the strength to keep going. He held me close and then he gave me the injection himself while I bawled like a baby. After that day my husband would always be on hand to give me the injections when I didn't feel courageous enough or when I was required to take them in my buttocks.

Aside from the mental and emotional stress there was also the financial stress. My husband and I spent over 4 million naira, in addition to 'the gift' and without calculating the multiple air commutes to and from Lagos and the personal expenses on drugs because after a while we started sourcing for our drugs from outside the hospital so we could buy them at a cheaper rate and at our own convenience. The hospital had been magnanimous enough to subsidize some of the services, so the 4 million naira listed above was a discounted price. We were out of our league, but God saw us through. A friend of mine had been led to give me a monetary gift which was timely because it helped me pay for a drug just when we were cleaned out. At another time God repeated this miracle of provision with my husband's friend giving us a monetary gift right on time. We never had to borrow even though I was a mid-level civil servant and my husband an early-stage entrepreneur. I kept asking them at the hospital to give us our entire bill so we could better plan but it was like every time we showed up for a clinic appointment, a new bill which ran into hundreds of thousands of naira showed up. One day I had been giving a bill of almost a million naira out of the blue and I tried calling my husband because I only had three hundred thousand naira in all my accounts combined and he wasn't picking his calls. I must have called him a million times. Dear hubby was in dream land, taking a heavenly and very rare mid-day nap while I endured the meaningful looks from the pharmacist as she waited for me to pay up. I called my mum to help pending when I could reach my husband and she sent someone to the bank to immediately do a transfer. While I was waiting for the credit alert and with my husband still not responding to his phone calls and messages I didn't know when I broke down in tears at the hospital lobby. It wasn't fair that they kept springing unexpected bills at me without any fore warning. I was angry that they didn't care that I earned a salary at the end of the month and didn't give me an opportunity to plan or even a straight answer about the total costs every time I asked and trust me, I was that patient that asked every single time. I had to be taken into the nurse's room to be consoled. I really felt stretched thin. It wasn't the first time I was crying at the hospital. The first time had been in the toilet after I had heard I had to do surgery. My husband's phone had been unreachable and one of my friends had to talk me through my tears back to a place of hope and strength. My mother who had accompanied me to the hospital had started calling my name and banging on the toilet door after some minutes after asking the nurses repeatedly for my whereabouts. She said she had been praying and she sensed in her spirit that I was somewhere crying. When she couldn't shake off the feeling, she had gone to look for me.

During the cycle, I had to travel to South Africa for an important event. I had to cancel two all-expenses paid business trips to Ghana and Senegal because of the cycle but the South African trip had come earlier on in the cycle before I was banned from travelling by my doctors. At the time of the trip, I was on injections on the clock. I had to take an injection at 8pm compulsorily every day regardless of where I was. On the day of my trip, my mom and I had frantically driven round Lagos trying to find a thermos bag because two of my injections needed to be always kept cold. We finally found a sturdy, affordable one in a shopping mall. I got to the airport, luggage in tow and drug carrier bag in my other hand. I had a cover letter from my doctor stating why I had to carry drugs and what drugs I had with me (very essential for travel), but it didn't stop me from feeling a little anxious. I had heard the stories about people being harassed and delayed unduly for all manner of reasons and I felt like my 'uncommon' drugs could make me a target especially since I was traveling alone. I prayed to God to grant me peace and favor and proceeded to the airport security point. My bags were immediately flagged after passing through the scanner and my heart sank. I rehearsed my explanation in my mind and instructed myself to stay calm. I almost laughed out loud when the officer in front of the scanning machine said I had a fork in my bag. Out came the fork with a brief apology and then the woman who searched the bag asked me what I had in my little carry on. I told her it was medication and she asked me what they were for. I told her and she proceeded to tell me how she had four children and she would pray for God to answer my prayers. I thanked her and left her with a little parting gift. My next dilemma occurred when the clock struck 8 and I was in the departure lounge and had to carry all my bags to the toilet to give myself the injections. It was clumsy and I was afraid of contamination or of someone wondering why I was in the toilet for so long. I feared that someone would discover me with all the drugs and needles and alert the drug enforcement agents that I was a junky. God was in control, and I gave myself the injections without incident or drama. Finally, when I was about to get on the plane there was one more search of our bags and I noticed an aggressive woman and a gentler man. I prayed that the man would be the one to search my hand luggage. God again heard my prayers and he searched it, zipping open and shut my drug bag with minimal interest and without questions even though it had ice cubes in Ziploc bags, syringes, needles and drugs. When I was walking away, I heard the woman call out to me to come back. I asked why and she said to be searched and before I could retort, the man spoke up that he had already searched me. I smiled a grateful smile and boarded the plane.

In South Africa, I timed my trips to ensure I was always home on or before 8pm and once had to miss evening service and at another time miss an interesting night market because of my drugs. One evening my friend and I had an important engagement at the U.S embassy in Pretoria and had to drive there from Johannesburg. The program ended late, and I was in my friend's car on the trip back when the clock struck 8. I had to pull up my dress and pull down my tight and panties to be able to get at my lower abdomen for my nightly jabs. I looked ridiculous, my body was clumsily contorted in a car seat, and I did it practically in the dark. It was quite an adventure albeit uncomfortable. On my trip back I didn't want any stories so as soon as I got to border control, I declared my drugs. The officer wasn't even moved, didn't read the letter and didn't ask me questions. Well better safe than sorry. While I was in midair enroute Nigeria, the clock struck 8pm and I had to carry my drug bag into the plane toilet to do my usual. Just after withdrawing the first drug in the syringe, the seat belt sign came back on, and the pilot announced some turbulence. There I was, needle in hand, plane vibrating and shaking anyhow and having no choice but to forge on because my injections were time bound. I was able to inject myself and return to my seat though the whole process took longer than usual, and I was a bit shaken up after. I got to my seat and congratulated myself with a couple of bars of duty-free chocolate (don't judge). I was steadily doing things I would never have imagined myself able to do and the thought was scary but exhilarating. He certainly kept true to His promise- Have I not commanded you? Be strong and courageous. Do not be afraid; do not be discouraged, for the Lord your God will be with you wherever you go (Joshua 1:19).

On my way back home, I had checked in all my luggage including the drugs arranged carefully around ice filled Ziplocs and frozen bottles of water and told them to put a fragile sign on them. I showed them the letter and explained what was in the bags and they assured me I was good to go only for me to be snapped out of my reverie at the departure lounge when I heard my name over the public address system. They needed me to report to their counter immediately. As I walked towards the exit gate, I felt scores of eyes on my back probably judging me, already concluding. I was ushered into a back room where the bags where scanned and there was a stern-faced female officer sitting behind the monitor. She asked me what was in my bag. I calmly explained to her about my drugs and the need to keep them cold and then she peered into the bag and read the doctor's cover letter. Her voice was considerably softer and quite soothing when she bade me farewell and good luck. At work, things weren't so rosy either. My leave letter mysteriously disappeared so my leave was cancelled, and I was given call duty even though they were privy to what I was going through but even though I shed quite a few frustrated tears and got really worked up over the apparent insensitivity of some of the parties involved, God still gave me divine favor with the most unlikely people and turned everything around for my good.

There were some not so bad times like when a lot of my blood was taken and spun in a centrifuge so they could extract plasma rich protein to inject in my womb. It was all part of the process of preparing my womb and after the uncomfortable, just bearable procedure I was given the rest of the PRP for my face. They told me that it worked wonders for the skin and people paid a lot of money for it. That night after my injections, I had a PRP facial. It felt weird slathering it all over my face almost like I was putting urine on my face (same color and consistency basically). Not sure if it worked though.

Then came the day for egg retrieval. I was asked to not use deodorant, body lotion, makeup, or perfume. Another epidural was done (no panic attacks this time because the anesthetist decided to give me the atropine injection before starting the procedure, genius!) and then the retrieval. My husband had given his sperm earlier that morning. That day we went home and prayed like we never had before. The hospital had said they would contact us. On the 2nd day after the egg retrieval the embryologist called to tell me that we had 3 embryos and they needed us to decide about whether we wanted them transferred on day 3 or wanted to wait till day 5. I asked him what the pros and cons were, and he said not all embryos would survive till day 5 so if we waited till day 5, we may not have any embryo to put in the womb. He also said that since the womb was a better house for them than the incubator, a day 3 embryo which may not have survived in an incubator still had a chance if it was in the womb. It was a tough decision and we had less than 10 minutes to make up our minds so that they could 'plan'. I called my friend, the one who had given us the gift. She had coincidentally been trying to call me while I was on the phone with the embryologist. She told me that they usually graded the embryos and if the embryos were a high grade, I could wait till day 5 but if they were a lower grade, I should have them transferred on day 3. I called the embryologist back and he said grading would not be done till the morning of day 3 so we might as well come to the hospital prepared just in case. That night again my husband and I prayed like we hadn't prayed in a long time. I had been praying along with sisters in the war room organized by a woman on her Instagram page and her prayers were always timely and relevant for the situations in my life especially during this cycle. I set my alarm for midnight and would wake hubby up to join me and would keep on even when his silent breathing showed that he was praying in his dreams. I would pray till I dozed off and wake up several times in the night to keep praying till I got to the last prayer post. The war room was usually only on Fridays but on the day of my egg retrieval, she had received a revelation to have the war room with fasting every day for two weeks. The next morning, we got to the hospital on time and waited for news about our embryos. The grading was done, and we were informed that two were a grade A to B and the last one was a grade B to C. We decided to wait for day 5 and the nurse was relieved, she mentioned that there was no embryo glue because of the short notice and if we had insisted on a day 3 transfer, they would have done it without the embryo glue which may have further impacted on our chances. So, we had two more days to wait and pray.

I held on to the promise made to Sarah, reminding myself than nothing was too hard for God. (Is anything too hard for the Lord? I will return to you at the appointed time next year, and Sarah will have a son- Genesis 18:14). I kept confessing that I would not be anxious about this IVF, for I had a favorable outcome, by prayer and petition, with thanksgiving, I had presented my requests to God. And the peace of God, which transcends all understanding, would guard my heart and my mind and my womb and my babies in Christ Jesus. Everyone who loved us and knew about what we were going through was praying for us. My friends were praying, our family was praying, our brethren in the Lord and pastors were praying. It had been seven long years and a collective cry was going up to heaven from different corners of the world for us. I sowed seeds where a seed was asked of me, and I made confessions about what I wanted to see in my life several times a day. The prayer circle was also on every hour on my behalf, and I felt so much peace. On the day of the embryo transfer, hubby and I arrived the hospital full of expectations and a little anxious. We were made to wait for hours during which hubby, and I watched two hilarious movies on Netflix. We were trying hard not to feed our fear and tried to keep the mood light. The doctor and embryologist explained that the reason for the wait was that they had been hoping that the third embryo would catch up, but it hadn't. They didn't want to put it in with its siblings because if it didn't make it, it might release chemicals in the womb that could affect the other two healthy embryos negatively. So, two healthy embryos were shown to me on the monitor, retrieved and put into my womb and then the doctor and nurse proceeded to pray for me and my husband and for the embryos in our womb. The prayer touched me deeply and sincerely. There's nothing quite like going to a faith-based hospital. Commit thy way unto the Lord; trust also in him; and he shall bring it to pass (Psalms 37:5). The doctor wasn't taken any chances. By committing the procedure into God's hands, she was increasing the odds in our favor! I was asked to remain on my back for about 45 minutes and then we were allowed to go home. We were advised to abstain from sex till they gave a go ahead and I was started on some new medication and injections which I was to continue for the next couple of weeks. We were also told that they would be in touch and that was how I left the hospital with two five-day old embryos in my womb. The next step would be a two week wait and then 'the test'. If ye abide in me, and my words abide in you, ye shall ask what ye will, and it shall be done unto you (John 15:7). We had some more asking to do!

Prayer

Dear Lord, you said in Proverbs 16:3 that we should commit to you whatever we do, and you will establish our plans. Thank you for ordering our steps and directing our path. Thank you for giving us peace during this fertility journey and for always providing answers and a way of escape in difficult situations. Thank you for the people you have placed in our lives to uphold us in prayers and strengthen our faith. Thank you for your continual provision and finally thank you for the testimony that awaits at the end of this journey in Jesus' name, Amen.

Action Point

Go to a new page in your Gratitude Journal and write out a list of specific miracles no matter how unspectacular that you have been blessed with in your fertility pursuits. When we are thankful, it delights God to bless us some more.

CHAPTER SEVEN

Success

The two weeks after the embryo transfer flew by. I stayed home, mostly inactive, taking my drugs and injections and joining the war room midnight prayers every night. During that period, I read part of a book by Andrew Wommack, 'Don't limit God' and I realized that I was guilty of limiting God with my thoughts and words. I would say 'if the Lord wills...' so that if it didn't go as planned, I could excuse my disappointment by saying 'it wasn't God's will. Well Brother Andrew wanted me to know that God had freely given me all things and no good thing would He withhold from me. My prayers took on a new boldness. My requests were non-negotiable. As long as they were in line with God's word there was no reason on earth why He should say NO. Jesus asked once in Matthew 7:9, 'which of you if your son asks for bread will give him a stone or for fish will give him a snake? If you who are evil know how to give good gifts to your children, how much more will your Father in Heaven give good gifts to those who ask him!' I certainly wasn't going to entertain the possibility of a no. I had gone through too much to get to this point and I believed that it all happened for a purpose- to bring me to an expected end. Indeed, I was on the mountain top! During the two weeks wait, a friend of mine who had been earnestly praying for me and encouraging me called to tell me she had an awful dream about me in which I was being attacked and she had to tell the women to back off that I was pregnant. I prayed against it though I honestly would have preferred she hadn't told me. I was also facing some work-related challenges at work and being punished for not turning in some non- essential reports even though the faculty was aware of my current situation but none of these things bothered me. From experience, I knew that when things get really hot it meant my breakthrough had already arrived. I was expectant and I could feel the miracle charging up my atmosphere.

The hospital called on my husband's birthday that since I couldn't be in Lagos for my appointment due to my work commitments, I was to go do a test that very day at a laboratory. The test had two parts to it. A qualitative test that would read 'pregnant or not pregnant' and a quantitative test that would measure exactly how much of the beta HCG pregnancy hormone I had in my blood. I was torn. I didn't want to do such a sensitive test on my husband's birthday, but I realized it could turn out to be the best birthday present ever, since we had never been pregnant. I suddenly felt anxious, I had descended from the mountain top, and it was time to see if my faith held water in the light of real-life circumstances. My husband and I drove to a new high-tech laboratory where they said the qualitative test would come out after a couple of hours, but the quantitative test would take some days. I did the tests, and I gave them my email address to mail the results to me as soon as they were ready. Some hours later I was sitting on the toilet flipping through my messages when the email came in. My heart began to beat fast, and I opened the email and waited for the contents to pop up. I scrolled down and saw the big, fat NEGATIVE. My spirit immediately rejected the result. I didn't believe it for a second. I dressed up and said nothing. I wasn't about to ruin my husband's day with a lie from the devil! I didn't know what I was going to tell him when he asked about the result, but I certainly knew it was not my result. The baker delivered my husband's cake and we drove to his pharmacy since he had chosen to celebrate with his staff. All through my cheeriness was forced and this thankfully went unnoticed. At the pharmacy, I sent a message to my spiritual mentor telling her what the result read and how I didn't believe it. She agreed with me that it was not our result and encouraged me to stand in the faith. The hospital called twice, wanting to know the result but I didn't answer the phone. My friend called to ask if I had done the test and I told her 'soon'. I wasn't ready to deal with the world yet. Not until my husband and I were on the same page- God's page!

On the drive back, my husband had asked about the test, and I told him I had received it. He was surprised and asked when I received it and why I hadn't informed him earlier. I told him in as calm a voice as I could muster that I didn't believe the result. I proceeded to encourage him, and my voice broke a couple of times as I struggled with tears while I spoke as strongly as I could that God would not bring us this far to leave us. I sent a message to the hospital that the qualitative was negative and I didn't want any phone calls and if they had any important information to pass across, they should send a message. The nurse replied that we would wait for the quantitative result just to be sure but that I was not to stop my medication. The very next day around the same time as the previous day and with me surprisingly sitting on the toilet, I received the second email. The quantitative result that was supposed to not be ready till three days after, was ready and it read 16! 16 may not seem like a large number but it was a miracle, my first conception miracle! Medically, a figure less than 5 is non-pregnant, 6-24 is borderline and requires retesting within 72 hours and greater than 25 is pregnant. The qualitative result was set to read values from 25 which was why it had turned up negative. I was so happy. I knew that this was a definite sign that I was winning this battle. It reminded me of the story in the bible when Elisha asked his servant to go and look at the clouds for rain and he kept checking and seeing nothing and then he saw a very small cloud the size of a man's hand and that was all the sign Elisha needed, soon there was thunderous rain after years of drought (1 Kings 18:41- 46). My phone rang just after sharing the good news with my husband and it was a counsellor from the hospital calling to help me with the grief process. I was momentarily super impressed because most hospitals cut you off abruptly when the procedure doesn't work, they usually only call months later to ask if you are ready for another procedure because they are shamelessly only concerned about the money. I cut her short excitedly and told her to tell the nurse the news. Soon, the nurse called, and we praised God together. She told me to repeat the test at a more standard, well renown laboratory after 48 hours as HCG levels were supposed to at least double after 48 hours in a healthy pregnancy.

For the next two days, I worshipped and confessed positively, my closest friends and my prayer circle were praying for me. I went online to check what value my beta HCG was supposed to be for the weeks pregnant I was and realized it needed to comfortably be a 3-digit figure. I prayed in line with that telling God that I didn't want a doubling (32 was still low), I wanted 3 figures. I repeated the test, and I was informed that the result would be ready in 2 days. The result came in on a Monday morning and lo and behold it was 109.26! I got my 3 figures!!! God is super awesome, and I cried, and hubby and I worshipped him and then we called the hospital and the staff screamed and jubilated (we could hear the noise in the background) and then I called my closest friends and family. It was a miracle, and we were overwhelmed with His goodness. My siblings cried, I still have picture evidence of their red eyes and grateful tears while at work, two of my closest friends cried. One had told me specifically when I told her about the first HCG result that God would take me from borderline pregnant to over-pregnant and she was so excited, the other had boldly declared to me weeks before that I would carry my babies in my womb, and she couldn't hold back the tears. Another of my friends almost screamed at a work meeting, he had been earnestly praying for me for a while and was overwhelmed. One of my friends immediately sent me her copy of the phenomenal book by Jennifer Polimino and Carolyn Warren, 'Praying through your pregnancy'. She was heavily pregnant and super excited for me. Earlier on in the cycle, she had prayed with me for a couple of days at midnight that the cycle would be successful. I really appreciated her prayers because we lived on two separate continents in different time zones, but we made it work. I had a list of other people close to my heart that I was eager to spill the beans to, but my family cautioned that I keep the news to myself going forward. Still, I went on ahead to tell my nearest and dearest who had upheld me in prayers, when they asked that it was going well, and they should keep praying. I was careful not to shut out any well-wishers despite not being able to give out full details. I also shared the testimony with the sister who organized the war room as it had really helped my prayer life and we blessed God for His faithfulness. I hadn't been attending physical church for a while just online church although my pastors were aware of my current situation and kept me in their prayers, I felt like I needed to 'hide' myself like Elizabeth did (Luke 1:24) not because I was afraid but because I wanted my testimony to announce itself without speculation or avenue for seeds of doubt. It was still so new to me that I didn't want to have to talk about it or explain why I didn't want to come out for fruit of the womb prayers or give any explanations about why I had put on so much weight all of a sudden (hormones from the IVF cycle + hormones after the cycle + hormones of early pregnancy).

A week later, I was asked to do my first ultrasound scan and hubby and I went to a new diagnostic center in town. The radiologist looked and said he couldn't see anything. I was confused and upset but I laughed it off as another film trick by the devil in a war I had already won. I spoke to my spiritual mentor, and she told me in no uncertain terms that the victory was won, and I shouldn't be moved. My doctor said she wanted me to travel to Lagos so she could scan me herself. She had two fears- 1. That I may have miscarried and 2. I may have an ectopic pregnancy (when the baby is growing outside the womb, it's an emergency and potentially life threatening). She asked me to do a repeat quantitative beta HCG test and a home pregnancy test. If the HCG test was still rising and a home pregnancy test positive, then I was still pregnant. I hadn't had any of the usual signs of miscarriage and more importantly it was my firm belief that I would not miscarry because the bible clearly stated that none shall miscarry or cast their young before time (Exodus 23:26). If I had waited 7 years to be pregnant for the very first time, those children in my womb were going to live a long and fulfilled life. I had not done a home pregnancy test not even after I got the positive blood pregnancy test, not even when my husband asked that he wanted one as a keepsake. The thing about it is that no matter how strong you are, the wait changes you. I wouldn't call it fear because I already had confirmed with more advanced tests that I was pregnant. It was more like revisiting a dark place. I had gotten so many negative urine pregnancy tests in the years I had been married and never one positive that it haunted me a little that the first time I was compelled to do the home pregnancy test was after a radiologist said he didn't see anything in my womb. I was scared and I immediately cast all my cares to God. Early the next morning I said a quick prayer and peed on the stick then quickly put it aside, unwilling to look. I finally picked up the clear blue pregnancy test and there it was clear as day 'pregnant'. I had used the other two sticks in the pack, months beforehand they had been negative, and I vaguely remembered praying back then over the last stick and here was God fulfilling His word yet again. I wasn't proud that I had had a moment of weakness with my faith, but I was grateful for a compassionate and patient Father and my faith was revived. My husband wasn't in the least bit surprised. He teased me about my fear which was why I had denied him his pregnancy stick days before and assured me that I was pregnant, and nothing was going to change that. Later that day I went to do the repeat beta HCG test. I specifically told God that this time I wanted a four-digit figure. The next morning the result was sent to my email, and it read 1,195.30. A whooping tenfold increase! I relaxed and decided to bask in God's rest as the story continued to unfold.

I was asked to take an intralipid infusion that was sent down from the hospital some days after the scan. There was no one available to set the line for me, so I had done it myself with the aid of my phone torch since the power was out. I had gotten the line and then when my husband returned from work, he helped me put it up. I remember commenting that the intralipid looked different from the one I took in Lagos and my husband had asked me why there was a saline infusion in the box. I told him I thought it was included just in case I had a reaction and needed to be resuscitated. All this was happening in my living room at night. I took the infusion without incidence and even sped it up a little when I got tired of lying down only for the nurse to tell me two days later over the phone that she hoped I didn't have any issues diluting the intralipid before administration! Diluting?!! No wonder it looked different. Apparently, I had taken the concentrated version and yet I had not had an adverse reaction. I was so grateful to God for keeping His promises and protecting me from inadvertent danger. The bible says even if we drink deadly poison, it will not hurt us at all (Mark 16:18). One of my closest friends that I had shared the testimony with had after congratulating me, unknowingly sowed a seed of doubt by saying 'make sure you check the HCG again to ensure it is rising'. I hadn't thought much of it at the time but when I was asked to repeat the beta HCG when the scan turned up negative, her words kept replaying in my mind and caused me untold grief. I remembered some years back my period had been late, and I had told this same friend that I felt I was pregnant, and she had said 'don't get your hopes up, it may just be stress' and those words back then had sowed seeds of doubt in my heart and soon after the period had come. I didn't blame her for being 'realistic' but when you are walking in faith, a realistic word may just be sugar coating doubt and the roots run deep. Faith does not rely on our senses or perception. When the repeat HCG result came out with a positive increase, I told her because I wanted to tie up the loose end. Doubt would not be entertained in this journey! Sometimes doubt can piggyback on the words of a close friend and it's the reason Jesus rebuked Peter (Mark 8:33). Peter thought he was looking out for Jesus, but his words were not in line with God's will. I learned to recognize and reject words that planted doubt regardless of how familiar the lips from whence they came.

I called the hospital, and they were pleased with the results. They asked me to come to Lagos as soon as I could and not to stop my medication. My body was gradually easing into morning sickness, not dramatic but some nausea, a lot of fatigue and unplanned sleep, an acute sense of smell and mutant taste buds. I was happy. It'd been a long road and God had finally come through for me. My EDD had been calculated to be March 2nd, 2020, if I was carrying one child but I wanted triplets. I felt like multiples were my due since I had waited so long. I was filled with so much joy but also a bit of trepidation. It was a long journey ahead and I had only taken the first step and of course occasionally there was the niggling doubt about the scan result. I had scanned enough women to know what I expected to see at 5 and a half weeks, but I attributed it to the fibroids I still had or poor technique. My husband felt perhaps the scan had been done too early. Whatever it was the devil couldn't win this, nothing was tainting my success. Jesus had finally come through for me!

Prayer

Dear Father, thank you for honoring your word and for making a way where there seems to be no way. Please help us to trust in your goodness when the devil tries to mar our blessings and help us to trust in your plan for our lives because no one can love us the way you do. Amen

Action plans

1. What negative thing is the devil saying about your life or health? What does the bible say about that situation? Whose report will you believe?

2. Do not let words contrary to what God is doing in your life proceed out of your mouth! Refrain from negative communication.

3. Keep rejoicing even when you see things that are contrary to what you are asking God for, it might just be a smoke screen!

CHAPTER EIGHT
Survivor Guilt

Survivor guilt is a psychological condition that occurs when a person feels guilty for surviving or 'escaping' a traumatic event when others have not. A lot of women who have conceived after waiting for a long time have experienced survivor guilt. They have formed firm friendships with other women who are also in waiting and then suddenly have to decamp. Getting pregnant becomes a bittersweet experience, because it comes with a twinge of guilt they can't shake off. They don't know how to act around these women anymore. They worry that their joyful exuberance and protruding bellies may be putting salt in their friends' wounds. Sometimes this guilt is further compounded by her friend's inability to move past her personal feelings of sadness over her unchanging situation and be happy for her. Sometimes the guilt is worsened by her desire to 'hide' her new status which may be born out of fear, mistrust, and paranoia or just in obedience to an instruction from someone else or above.

A friend of mine had called me the year before, out of the blue in tears that she had just lost her pregnancy and I experienced a torrid mix of unexpected emotions. I was shocked and confused because I had seen her almost every day prior to that and had no clue that she was pregnant even though we had both been in waiting for a while. I felt sad and heartbroken because she had lost something she had wanted for so long. I felt hurt because she hadn't trusted me enough to confide in me till she needed a shoulder to cry on. For the time being I put my feelings aside and was there for her. I was everything she needed me to be. It didn't take too long however, to realize she wasn't the only one that needed comforting. I called my mom to unburden my chest and she told me it was usual for some friends not to tell each other sensitive stuff like this because of our African culture and the 'you don't know who is really happy for you' mentality and that maybe the couple had reasons for keeping it in and I shouldn't let it affect me. But it wasn't what I wanted to hear. All my other friends had told me the news as soon as they peed on the stick and this friend had shed tears more than once that some other friend of hers had excluded her from the baby announcement and since some of her inner circle knew about it, I felt I had been deliberately excluded. I called up one of my oldest friends to whine about it and as I was going on and on about the seeming betrayal, I let it slip that all that time I had confided in this friend about the procedure I had done, and she had never once felt the need to trade her own secret and voila, the next instance something unexpected happened. My dear friend cut me short and asked when I had the procedure done. I told her and then it dawned on me that I was just as guilty, I felt the embarrassment creep up my neck. I had kept the details from my friend even though she had initially suggested it and asked me about it once or twice. I hastily replied that I wanted to be sure the procedure had worked and was waiting for the right time to break the 'good' news which unfortunately never came. I tried to convince her that I hadn't excluded her for any negative reason and that it was just more convenient to tell my other friend because she was going through the same issues that I was and in close proximity. Right then it occurred to me that I had been feeling hurt and betrayed when I had done the same thing to my other friend! Thankfully this friend had no ill feelings towards me, and she helped me gain important perspective and let go of any hurt feelings I may have harbored towards my other friend.

So many friendships have had bad blood mar them because one friend hid a pregnancy or some other good news from the other. Reasons for doing this have ranged from protecting their friend's feelings, preventing jealousy or bad blood, protecting good news from frenemies or just to keep the news private till it's established but most times they inadvertently hurt someone who had only good intentions towards them, someone who may have labored in prayers for her alongside her own requests and if that someone is another woman in waiting then the pain is raw and unending because of the other factors at play. The friend usually doesn't know which of the above reasons you had for excluding her and many times emotions make people assume the worst. I have consoled different women in waiting who cried their eyes out because a close friend hid the news of her pregnancy from them. Survivor guilt seems to be more common than we would expect.

An acquaintance told me a story of how she and her best friend went for an IVF cycle together at the same hospital and her best friend conceived with twins but her own procedure hadn't worked and eventually the two longtime friends had gone their separate ways. She said her friend started acting funny and treating her weird and I couldn't help thinking perhaps her friend also had survivor guilt. I always viewed survivor guilt from the other side of the divide till I got pregnant. I doubted that it was a real thing and had made up my mind not to make any of my friends feel bad by shutting them out when the time came but managing my personal story seemed trickier and more sensitive than I imagined when the shoe was on the other foot! It was easy letting my inner circle know that I was doing an IVF simply because I wanted to do things differently the second time. The first time had been shrouded in secrecy and well it hadn't worked. This time I wanted them praying and supporting me and honestly it made the cycle so much easier. After I got a positive result, I experienced three distinct emotions. The first was excitement. It was the first time I had ever been pregnant, and I wanted to tell everyone and scream it from the rooftops. The second emotion was fear- what if the pregnancy developed complications? What if I announced it and it didn't progress? It made me want to limit the number of people that knew about it till I was totally in the clear. I heard a word in my spirit- when the Lord gives you this pregnancy you will not hide it in fear, you will do everything you want to do. I made a conscious effort to replace fear with faith. The third emotion surprised me. I felt survivor's guilt and agonized about how and when to break the news to my other friends in waiting. I realized that it was easier to break the news to my friends who already had kids. I was determined to rise above the third emotion because of my personal experience being on the receiving end. I thought about the times friends had shared their pregnancy announcements with me and how genuinely happy I had been for them even though I was still waiting, and it occurred to me that others would be just as happy for me and that even if they experienced some sadness about their own personal situation, they would like I had, put it aside and be there for me and rejoice with me.

One of my friends in waiting who knew I had gone for the IVF procedure sent me a message one day soon after my beta HCG came out as positive. She said she had dreamed about me that I was pregnant. At that point I knew I had two choices, to say 'amen' and change the topic or to confide in her. I felt a bit of anxiety because I hadn't yet done a comparison HCG to make sure it was rising appropriately neither had I done a scan. I felt it might be too early but I didn't want to risk her getting hurt and so I told her the IVF had gone well and I was waiting to do all the confirmation tests before announcing. She gave me a series of happy emojis, and we ended on a good note, yet I felt so terribly guilty for the rest of that day and couldn't be sure how she had received the news. I couldn't understand why I was feeling guilty and even caught myself rehearsing conversations with her in my head. I felt like I needed to offer her an explanation for why this IVF had worked when she had done several which had failed, I felt like I needed to comfort her even though it was unsolicited. Survivor guilt can be quite complex but recognizing it is the first step to controlling it. Having a baby after waiting is a miracle, a thing of joy. You shouldn't be feeling guilty, no you need to shake off the guilt and instead offer support to your friends in waiting and involve them as much as you can in the pregnancy planning- as much as you both are comfortable with. A few years ago, a friend of mine who had been the only other woman waiting in my faculty missed her period for a few days. She rushed to tell me excitedly and we screamed about it, and I had been so happy. I had convinced her to go and do a blood pregnancy test and when she got a positive, she had come straight to my house to share the good news. I experienced her pregnancy with her and the birth of her son and even on her son's birthday she gave me children party packs for my children who were still on the way. There is no way of knowing if she had survivor guilt at any point in time, but she did not let it get in the way of our friendship. Take advantage of every opportunity to lift someone else up because one day you may need lifting.

So how do you control the dissemination of your private affairs without sacrificing a good friend on the altar of secrecy? Here are three points to note. These points don't apply if you deliberately excluded the person for any reason. The first is to be consistent. Let your friend know exactly what place she occupies in your life. Every person has different circles of friends. If you have two best friends, don't tell one and leave the other out unless it is a known fact that you are closer to one of them. If you tell only your inner circle your secret, a friend in the outer circle wouldn't feel excluded unless you had given her reason to believe that she was part of your inner circle or she had shared similar sensitive information with you in the past. The second is to be sensitive. Don't assume that your friend understands why she wasn't included. Take out time to explain to her and to gently tackle how she may be feeling. Invest more time, attention and love into the relationship so that you restore the balance that was there before the big reveal and so that she is assured that she wasn't excluded for a negative reason. This may take time, don't be in a hurry to move on unless you are sure she has. The third is to be fair. The world is so intertwined that many times we get as good as we give. If you are a private person, then don't get mad if someone else keeps their information private. If you planned to keep the information private but a couple of people already know about it, close the gap by telling the people who are important to you rather than risking someone in your inner circle hearing it from a random person outside or finding out she was one of the few people who didn't know. Remember gist gets around fast.

Life isn't static. We will always have our own secrets and not be privy to someone else's. Even though we may be inadvertently or intentionally excluded from certain circles of trust, we must be careful not to point fingers for with someone else we may have unwittingly crossed the same line. People have different characters and if you choose to be friends with a secretive person, you must own this and not get upset when the person is just being herself. You must also understand that some secrets are kept out of fear of past personal failures (they don't want to jinx it) and not fear of what you can or can't do to ruin it. If you choose to keep a secret, do it for your own reasons and not because of advice from some random third party who doesn't understand the depth of your friendship and has made you suspicious of the very people you have trusted during your wait. Your friend knows you and as a result can anticipate your reactions and odd patterns of behavior hurt even more.

If you have been plagued with survivor guilt and as a result have compromised some meaningful friendships, don't sweep them under the carpet. Have a sit down with the person and talk about it. Never underestimate the power of forgiveness, love and understanding in mending broken friendships. Many women in waiting who have been hurt by a friend who hid a pregnancy from them confessed that an apology and talking things over would have been enough for them. Don't be quick to assume that people will not be able to handle your good news. Making excuses for them in your head or trying to protect someone who hasn't asked for your protection often leads to misplaced good intentions and unnecessary misunderstandings. One of my friends who was quite close to me when she was waiting, on two occasions informed me of the birth of her baby for the first time, weeks after the baby was born. Both times I had absolutely no idea she was pregnant. I sent heartfelt wishes both times and didn't pay it a second thought, but she must have felt I might be upset because she reached out to someone to find out if I was angry. It occurred to me that quite a few people believe that they have to walk on eggshells around women in waiting without realizing that many women in waiting just want to be treated like regular people without their affliction always getting the spotlight. Survivor guilt is definitely a thing but turn it into an avenue to lift others up and not an excuse to isolate yourself or hurt those dear to you.

Prayer

Lord, please help me to rejoice with those who rejoice and be a friend that sticks closer than a brother. Help me to overcome survivor guilt and to be understanding and supportive of my friends especially those still in waiting. Thank you for the gift of friendship and help me to be patient and understanding with all I hold dear in Jesus' name. Amen

Action Point

1. Have you ever had survivor guilt? Why did you have it and how did you overcome it?
2. Are there any friendships in your life that require mending? Would you be willing to take the first step?

CHAPTER NINE

Darkness

A week after my first ultrasound scan turned up empty, I was asked to repeat the scan again but somewhere else. I did, and the same thing happened. The radiologist said all he could see was a bulky womb with a thickened endometrial plate and some fibroids but again no baby. By now I was sick and tired of the games. He looked carefully for an ectopic pregnancy but couldn't find any in the usual places. I was torn, I felt doubt begin to creep in. I tried desperately to hold on to my faith, but my current reality kept distracting me. On my way home, over and over I prayed for the peace of God that passes all understanding to guard my mind and heart in Christ Jesus (Philippians 4:7). I knew my mind was a battlefield and I didn't want to lose the war. I didn't even tell anyone what was going on apart from my mom and one of my siblings. I certainly didn't need anyone worsening the doubt I was struggling with. My husband was strangely calm and unmoved. I didn't tell my spiritual mentor anything this time, I couldn't. I was ashamed that after all God had done for me up until this point, I could even still entertain the smallest doubt. I decided to make it my mission to restore my faith and I started a mini-fast, would search the scriptures, make confessions and talk to God. I let Him know how I was feeling and what my requests were and infused them with a healthy dose of gratitude. I knew He was going to do something big. I continued writing this book with no idea how the end would turn out, but I was trusting that since this book was a fulfilment of the vow, I made to Him if He would have mercy upon me and bless me with children then certainly there would be children before I walked the end of this path of obedience. God certainly kept His end of a bargain. The people who knew about my pregnancy would call me from time to time to ask if I was experiencing any pregnancy symptoms. Honestly, I didn't want to be sick, I had always prayed for an uneventful pregnancy, and I had an important exam in three months that required my full attention. I had breast tenderness and some fatigue but other than my acute sense of smell and new dislike for certain foods I still felt totally fine. The hospital asked me to come without fail to Lagos so they could do the ultrasound scan for me at their facility. Two of my closest friends had asked if I knew what I was having yet (singleton, twins, triplets etc.), I told one that I would let her know as soon as I knew and told the other person that I had an appointment with the doctors in Lagos the next weekend and would let him know afterwards. I didn't know what the doctors would see but I was certain that I was going to have a great testimony and gratitude on my lips after the hospital appointment. The night before my trip to Lagos I was plagued with the worst nausea I had ever experienced. I had to sleep with a bucket beside the bed and through the discomfort I would mutter thank you Jesus. I knew that God was in complete control and I was expectant of the unfolding of the next phase of the miracle that had already been dished out for me from Heaven.

I got to Lagos on a Friday evening and that night I joined the war room prayers and prayed fervently over my appointment the next day. The next day I was at the hospital right on time and soon it was time for the scan. The doctor scanned and re-scanned but couldn't see any evidence of a pregnancy within the womb or outside the womb. She asked me to go and do a repeat beta HCG test and I went to the lab to get my blood taken. The lab scientist told me the result would be ready in an hour and I settled down to wait. After an hour I went to meet her, and she said she had been asked to rerun the test. I knew something was up. My score was 6000! It wasn't skyrocketing but it was too high for a baby not to be found. I was subjected to another scan by another doctor, and she also didn't see anything. The diagnosis was pregnancy of unknown location and they needed to deliberate on the next line of action. During this time, I spoke to my spiritual mentor who was not buying the medical report for a second. Her faith was unwavering. My mother shared her faith. One of the doctors felt the safest option at this point was to take a medication to kill all fetal life- it was the medical treatment for an ectopic pregnancy even though it had not been proven beyond reasonable doubt that it was an ectopic. The second doctor felt since there were no symptoms or signs of an ectopic pregnancy, I should be closely monitored and report to a hospital at the slightest sign of pain, bleeding, dizziness or a reduction in my blood level (drop in packed cell volume). My friend asked me to get an independent opinion from a doctor at another hospital. The doctor said he saw a complex mass that looked to be in my left fallopian tube with what appeared to be surrounding blood clots. It wasn't a textbook case as there was no probe tenderness (pain felt when the ultrasound scan probe presses against the side where the mass is located), no gestational sac or fetus and no fluid in my pouch of Douglas. He called it a left sided ectopic pregnancy and wanted me to do an operation the next day which would cost a million naira and would entail the removal of the mass and my left fallopian tube. During the IVF egg stimulation phase, the doctors had noted that my right ovary did not respond as well to stimulation despite the high dosage of drugs. If this doctor removed my left tube, I would be stuck with a good left ovary without a tube and a not-so-great right ovary with a tube. It sounded like my fertility would be doomed. He said I could opt for the medical treatment but there was no guarantee that I wouldn't still require surgery. I thanked the doctor and told him we would be in touch. During this turmoil I was strangely at peace. I had briefed my parents and siblings and they had decided to fast and pray.

On our way home from the hospital my husband and I sang praises to God, we talked some, we prayed some and I cried a little. It was all so overwhelming. God could have stopped this at any point in time. Why

81

allow my friend to give me the gift? Why allow the IVF to be successful when the odds were against it working? Why give us a positive result after the qualitative pregnancy test said negative? Why not permit a miscarriage? We could both agree that we had no understanding of the events that were unfolding, and we would simply need to trust God. We came up with a spiritual and physical action plan. The physical action plan was in line with the expectant management and close monitoring the second doctor had recommended. In addition, we decided to taper the drugs I had been on instead of stopping abruptly as the hospital had recommended. I had been on high dose steroids, high dose hormones, high dose anticoagulants and high dose supplements for weeks and felt reducing the dosage gradually till I stopped them altogether was a much better transition. The spiritual action plan was to commence waiting on the Lord through fasting, prayer and worship. I was not going to die; I would not require an operation and I would not lose my fallopian tube! We contacted a gynecologist in Benin and told him about the events so he would be on standby. We sent a message to our Lagos doctor letting her know our decision and asking her to send us the prescription for the drug she had advised we take to remove the pregnancy. It wasn't in our immediate plans to take it, but we wanted to be prepared. We knew that God had a plan and all we had to do was align with it. He had seen the 20th of July long before we even decided to do an IVF. He had also seen the days and weeks after that and we decided to just trust Him. My success was not going to change to sorrow. It was the very first time I was getting a positive pregnancy test, my life and body would not pay the price for it! He had promised and He would fulfil it. The Lord said to me, "You have seen correctly, for I am watching to see that my word is fulfilled" (Jeremiah 1:12).

I was determined to stand on His word. I had heard enough testimonies to know I could change any report with prayers. Faith moves forward even when we don't have all the facts. Faith is the courage to move forward despite your fears. Faith moves forward amid fears. It wasn't about how I was feeling because as a medical doctor I knew just how unreliable feelings could be, it was about a knowing that was profound. Knowing however turned out to be the easy part, getting my rational thinking brain to not focus on the physical evidence right in front of me that was saying contrary things was the hard part and then I decided to just focus on Jesus. The same Jesus who looked at them and said, "With man this is impossible, but with God all things are possible" (Matthew 19:26). I needed to have the right attitude. Caleb trusted God to give Israel the land he promised them. "No misfortune is seen in Jacob, no misery observed in Israel. The Lord their God is with them; the shout of the King is among them (Numbers 23:21). I would stand firm and declare positive affirmations to combat the negative ones. Caleb declared, "We can certainly conquer it!" (Num. 13:30). The Lord answered Moses, "Is the Lord's arm too short? Now you will see whether or not what I say will come true for you" (Numbers 11:23). I knew He was a strategic God. Before we called, He had answered. He had planned all our days before we were born. We chose to reject every kind of evil (1 Thessalonians 5:22).

On our way back to Benin we had noticed the airplane was really small, but we shrugged it off. Only to get to the departure lounge and be informed that only half of the checked in luggage could be put on the plane and the rest would be arriving the next day. No prior warning so we could have removed essentials from our luggage. All my drugs were in my luggage including the ones which required refrigeration. Because it was a short flight, we had put them in a cooler with some ice but spending the night in an airport cargo room couldn't guarantee their preserved efficacy. I didn't know whether to laugh or cry. The hospital had asked me to stop the drugs immediately and I hadn't wanted to go cold turkey but now the airline company had made the decision for me. If it was another country, I would sue but for some reason we took a lot of these ineptitudes in our stride in Nigeria. We didn't hold anyone to higher standards. So, I got home that day with no medication, with a diagnosis I couldn't accept, fearing for the worst but hoping for the best. I desperately needed a miracle! I was not going to think about the fact that the doctors had sort of casually given me a death sentence. In my ten plus years of practicing medicine I knew, had treated and had heard of several women with ectopic pregnancies and delays usually affected their chances of living or dying but I wasn't going to worry about me. Worrying robs you of gratitude, it tramples on your faith, and it makes you despondent. When you look back at all the things you ever worried about, did the worrying help? Could you positively say thank God I worried? You can rest easy because of His promises; they will have no fear of bad news; their hearts are steadfast, trusting in the Lord (Psalm 112:7). I was instead going to pray for my babies. That they would be found. Jesus had said emphatically that, whatever you ask for in prayer, believe that you have received it, and it will be yours (Mark 11:24). Truly I tell you, if you have faith as small as a mustard seed, you can say to this mountain, 'Move from here to there,' and it will move. Nothing will be impossible for you" (Matthew 17:20). "'If you can'?" said Jesus. "Everything is possible for one who believes" (Mark 9:23). Jesus replied, "Truly I tell you, if you have faith and do not doubt, not only can you do what was done to the fig tree, but also you can say to this mountain, 'Go, throw yourself into the sea,' and it will be done. If you believe, you will receive whatever you ask for in prayer" (Matthew 21:21

The next day I had gone to check my beta HCG. The doctor had said that if it had doubled in 48 hours, it means it was a normal pregnancy and the intrauterine location would miraculously unfold but if it had increased but not doubled or started to decrease then an ectopic was likely and I was to take Methotrexate the injection which would end the baby's life and hopefully save mine. So many bible verses were flooding my Spirit. I was afraid but I was fighting fear with faith. My happy ending was the plan. The ending where I carried my babies to term and delivered them in peace. I was going to hold fast to my profession because that's what the bible had asked me to do. Let us hold fast the profession of our faith without wavering; for he is faithful that promised (Hebrews 10:23). Faithful is he that calleth you, who also will do it (1 Thessalonians 5:24). God is faithful and He wants us to activate our faith and starve our fears regardless of our human perception. Psalm 16:8 says I keep my eyes always on the Lord. It was a fierce battle, and I was not going to give in. My beta HCG result didn't come out till two days later and it turned out to be 8241, far from doubling. I was so disappointed I cried. Meanwhile I had been evading calls from anyone who was going to pressure me to take the medication and there suddenly were quite a number. I decided to do one more beta HCG test that morning and if it did not double, I would throw in the towel and accept God's confusing and very painful will. I prayed hard for a miracle and called all the men and women of God I know and close family to join me in prayers. This was on Wednesday the 24th of July 2019. I had just made some stew and put rice on the fire to boil when I picked up my phone and saw that another spiritual mentor of mine SL, had put up prayers against the spirit of death. I said those prayers fervently and afterwards went to check my rice. As I was leaving the kitchen, I started having some cramping in my lower abdomen. It was sudden and scary but mild and I sat down for a moment, thinking about what to do. I was home alone, and my husband had gone into town. I knew I needed to reach him and get him home urgently but calmly. I opted for a phone call instead of a message. His phone was busy, but he called back soon enough and told me he was already home and just parking the car. I went to urinate and when I wiped there was blood on the tissue. My whole life flashed in front of me. I couldn't believe this was happening. I took a deep breath and thought of the best-case scenario. I had gone cold turkey on very high doses of intramuscular and pessary progesterone so maybe it was a withdrawal bleed. I was afraid that the doctors would see me bleeding and wheel me straight into surgery and I desperately wanted to stay home but my husband wasn't having any of that. My plan to wait till Friday before acting had again been thwarted by circumstances or in retrospect an act of God.

We got to the hospital and there was a little delay seeing the doctor. By then I was sweating and feeling a little woozy. I hoped it was anxiety and not signs of something more foreboding. My husband was trying his best to be strong for me, the worry on his face was heartbreaking. My family and his were calling every second, worrying, praying. I heard him reassure each worried voice on the other end of the line. I wasn't interested in my phone. I asked to do an abdominal and transvaginal ultrasound scan while waiting. I told them I was a doctor and they allowed me to self-prescribe the tests. I wanted the doctor to have a recent scan to work with and more importantly I wanted to be sure I didn't have internal bleeding and if I did reduce the waiting time by doing the scan before instead of after the consultation. When I introduced myself to the radiologist as a medical colleague and told him the story about the pregnancy of unknown location, possibly ectopic and my newest symptoms, I knew he would not leave any stone unturned. I eventually got scanned by three radiologists and they were convinced that there was a mass in my left fallopian tube, and it looked like a gestational sac with a yolk sac (no fetus seen). There was also some fluid in the pouch of Douglas which showed a leak and pending rupture. I went in to see the doctor and he prescribed the methotrexate and wanted to admit me, but I declined promising that if I even felt the slightest discomfort I would return. He was doubtful that medical treatment would work because my beta HCG was so high but was willing to try because of the peculiarity of the situation.

We were allowed to take the injection home to administer it since my husband was an experienced pharmacist who had been the one administering injections to me for weeks prior to this event. We tried to stay strong for each other and in-between questioning why this was happening and expressing our misery were able to still give God thanks and ask for His help. The prayers had changed now. We wanted the injection to work so I wouldn't require surgery. Hubby vowed that he would never allow me to be subjected to what I had been through in the last couple of months ever again. As we prepared to take the injection to end the pregnancy, I got two messages that made me the more emotional. A lady I used to be friends with who had waited for the fruit of the womb for years and who had often been in my prayers even after we stopped being close had just delivered a son. The second message was a thank you message from a woman who had asked for prayers for a pregnancy that doctors had said was no longer viable and miscarrying. I had picked her prayer request during one of the war rooms and she was messaging me to express her gratitude for my prayers. God had answered her prayers and the pregnancy was not only now viable, but they had heard the baby's heartbeat. God had answered prayers about others that I had offered to Him but not my own personal prayers. I felt like I had asked Him for bread, and He had given me a stone, for fish and He had given me a snake. I was so sad, so broken and the tears flowed freely. I told my husband I wanted to administer the injection myself and he saw my determination and agreed. I wanted to be the one to pull the trigger. I had been on this walk, my body had been subjected to unimaginable pain and so many medications, it had experienced early pregnancy symptoms and the joy of new life and now it felt right that I do it. I didn't want to ever put the blame on anyone else in my darkest hours. I stabbed my thigh not even feeling the pain, eerily calm. I had been warned that I may have severe nausea and vomiting as a side effect, but I felt nothing as I lay on the bed unable to sleep. Thoughts of breaking bad news to all who had shared my testimony made me uneasy. I hated pity in any form, and I knew that a lot of tears still lay ahead. I tossed and turned because I remembered all the prayers and fasting and praise and the fact that God had probably being saying NO all along. I thought of my exams which were coming up in the next two months and wondered if I would be emotionally stable enough to read for them. The tears flowed freely from time to time, my husband's regular breathing as he slept beside me, my only succor. At least I wasn't alone. I read the encouraging words and testimonies close friends and family had shared with me. My sister had told me about a friend who had travelled to the US only to be birthed of a stillborn child and how she had wept but she was pregnant again. She had told me about another who had buried a child not knowing that God had already placed another in her womb. I knew we couldn't question God. He alone understood why He allowed such awful things to happen. It didn't stop me from feeling crushed. At around 4am, I glanced at my phone and the daily memory verse for my bible app caught my attention, boldly displayed on my screen. 'Our Lord, we belong to you. We tell you what worries us, and you won't let us fall- Psalm 55:22.' And then I heard Him speak. He told me how much He loved me, He told me He hadn't forgotten or forsaken me and that this was all part of His glorious plan. Before I drifted off to sleep there was a song in my Spirit. I knew I was going to be okay. I felt His peace wrap me around like a warm embrace. The road ahead didn't look easy, but I was going to have to trust in His goodness.

Prayer

Father we choose to trust you in times of turmoil and in times of pain. We choose to have faith especially when the situation seems hopeless. I keep my eyes focused on you because you uphold my right hand and keep me from being moved. I will stand firm on your promises because they are true. Guide us, protect us and lead us to calm resting places, away from the trouble and away from the pain. Help us not to worry and direct our paths at all times in Jesus' name.

Action Plan

When your heart is broken and you feel unimaginable pain, where do you run to for respite?

CHAPTER TEN

What If It Never Happens?

What if the children never come? A thought no woman who is waiting ever wants to entertain. A thought too heart breaking to consider but for some this ultimately becomes their reality. The bible says, 'none shall be barren' (Exodus 23:26) so why should I even have a chapter like this in my book? Well, the bible also says this in Hebrews 11:9, 'All of them pleased God because of their faith! But still they died without being given what had been promised'. So yes, sometimes it happens. Look at this chapter as not negating your faith but a guide to how to thrive if the wait is longer than you ever anticipated, or you never do get this one desire. God remains God! God has marked out your appointed times in history and where you will live (Acts 17:26). Every success, significance and influence you will ever have God has marked it out. He has given an appointed time for you to make history and has marked out where you will live and the boundaries of your land. So, trust in His timing and plan for your life.

After the first IVF didn't go as expected, it crossed my mind that what if God's final word on my situation was a NO? Would I still love Him? Would I still serve Him? Would I be disappointed in my big God? Would I be able to have faith in Him for other aspects of my life? Would I be able to move on and live a great life? Would I be bitter? Would I be able to sincerely tell others about God's abounding love and faithfulness? Would I be able to keep being happy for others who had an easy miracle of conception? Gosh, there were so many questions, and each was more haunting than the previous one. My ability to have children was somehow tied to the core of my Christian faith and it scared me. In Daniel 3: 17 and 18, Shadrach, Meshach and Abednego said these profound words to King Nebuchadnezzar, "If we are thrown into the blazing furnace, the God we serve is able to deliver us from it, and he will deliver us from your Majesty's hand. But even if he does not, we want you to know, Your Majesty that we will not serve your gods or worship the image of gold you have set up." These young men meant business. They were not going to compromise their faith even if God did not show up for them. How great was that? I realized that so many of us- myself included are in a bargaining relationship with God where we keep worshipping Him if He delivers on His own side of the bargain. God doesn't need us, we on the other hand cannot exist without Him.

I had made a promise to God on the 26th of February 2018 before the roller-coaster events in my life. I said "Give us children Lord, just like you promised. But like those three Hebrew boys in the fiery furnace, even if You do not, I will serve You. My life is Yours. Even if the Lord doesn't give me children, even if the Lord doesn't make me great, even if the Lord doesn't answer my prayers, I will still worship him forever for He is Almighty, and the unquestionable God so why worry about things only He can control?" Those who know your name trust in you, for you, Lord, have never forsaken those who seek you (Psalm 9:10). This woman was determined to serve God regardless of the outcome of the wait and she was doing it for three major reasons. The first reason was that God loved her more than she could ever love herself (Romans 8:35-39), the second reason was that He was careful to bring to pass every word He had spoken (Numbers 23:19) and finally, her third reason was that He was Her Abba Father and knew the end from the beginning (Isaiah 46:10). She was determined to stop worrying about the future. She wanted to start viewing the present as a gift! I decided to wait quietly like the scriptures said for His plan to unfold, 'let all that I am wait quietly before God, for my hope is in him' (Psalm 62:5). Believe what God says about you and what he has promised you regardless of what the majority of people (society, friends, and peers) might say about you or think.

My next action plan was to scratch my itch in other positive ways. Waiting is not the most pleasant experience and sometimes the longing for a child can become a monstrous itch you just need to scratch. Some people get tired of the endless waiting. They lose patience and shelve their deepest longing in a box labelled unattainable and make do with a more realistic albeit less satisfactory alternative. That doesn't have to be the case. Your pain can connect you with your purpose and you can scratch an itch in more satisfying and impactful ways. Our passion is often birthed from our pain. This book was birthed after a vow I made to God in the midst of my pain. A close friend of mine started her business after the pain she went through when her newborn baby had jaundice. The mission is always clear- to help other people who are going through what you went through. The bible says in 2 Corinthians 1:4 that God comforts and encourages us in every trouble so that we will be able to comfort and encourage those who are in any kind of trouble, with the comfort with which we ourselves are comforted by God. I scratched my itch for interacting with children in a private, meaningful way through an organization online where I could give money to needy children from all over the world and even have a relationship with them, it was called Compassion International and getting letters from the children and being an unobtrusive part of their lives warmed my heart.

I discussed adoption with my husband, not because I thought we immediately needed it but because it was a previously unexplored option. I did some research and found out that adoption was a hard, very long and emotionally draining process. The internet wasn't much help and there were horrific tales from other waiting women about the bureaucracy involved. One would have thought connecting a loving couple with a child in desperate need of loving parents would be encouraged and fast tracked but that was far from the case. The heart ache from a failed adoption process cut just as deep as that from a failed IVF and there was a long line of social workers, orphanage staff and people from child protective services as well as legal people between you and your future child. For some, it was a tedious but worthwhile journey as bringing a child into the home brought so much love and joy, and their addition had been associated with an unexplained opening of some women's wombs for conception as well as numerous other blessings. Some women opted for taking in a relative's child or being a 'big mummy or doting godmother' to a close friend or family's child to ease off the pressure and scratch the mothering itch and the gains were often similar. It helped to re-channel their love and bring them to a state of calm while they waited. Others cared for the children in their community, offering help in various ways including visits with food and clothing to local orphanages. These visits give a sense of fulfilment and warm the heart. Mother Theresa showed us that one didn't have to have biological children to be a mother of all.

Living life to the fullest when infertility has cast a dark shadow over your marriage and social life can be difficult, but you have to rise above it to thrive. Focus on what you already have. There is so much negativity in the world that if you only stopped for a second to appreciate what you already had, you would be filled with such gratitude. Sometimes the things we are waiting so earnestly for could change our lives irreversibly for the better and maybe for the worse so use the waiting time to strike off all the other things on your to-do list. A new baby may make getting that postgraduate degree more complicated so why don't you get it now. Children may put a dampener on your dreams to travel the world so why don't you do that now instead of wallowing? A larger family will not fix the intimacy issues you and your husband have at the moment and often couples who have been waiting for a while take their eyes off what's most important (each other) and instead focus on the perceived problem or lack. The first step would be to put aside all offense and make sure you and your spouse are on the same page. If mistakes have been made which have altered the peaceful balance of the home, do all that is in your power to right them including asking God to help you forgive where necessary. Unless your plan is to walk away from the marriage, there is never a good enough reason for sacrificing your marriage on the altar of infertility. Don't take each other for granted. Appreciate and celebrate even the littlest things. Let your spouse have no need for external validation. Pamper each other in the little things and the big things. Attend couples' retreats and counselling sessions where necessary. Make your relationship your priority.

What to do with all the excess time? Travel! See the world, explore. The change of scenery will not only do you a world of good, but the excitement and adventure will help with the bonding process with your spouse. Make a pact not to discuss fertility issues when on vacation and don't suck the fun out of intimacy with the ovulation monitors and period checkers. These holidays could help mend the unseen wounds that your everyday fertility routine have created. There are travel plans and staycations for every budget. Let these getaways be a treat for you both that you look forward to from time to time. Reignite the romance even while at home. Make your marriage fun. Have you allowed yourself let go where your appearance is concerned? Do you like what you see in the mirror? Does your husband like what he sees? Sarah and Rebekah were no strangers to waiting for a child, but they had something else in common. They were so attractive that kings and influential men desired them, and their husbands had to pretend they were blood relatives of their own wives because they feared for their lives (Genesis 20:2, Genesis 26:7). It takes a lot for a woman to catch a king's eye. Kings are known for wanting only the best and they have their fill of the most beautiful women. I imagine these women were not only beautiful, but they were well spoken, composed, dressed well, were properly groomed and had an irresistible aura around them. Does that describe how you used to be before you lost yourself in the wait and the highs and lows of the fertility journey?

Girl! You need to get your groove back on. You are first of all your husband's woman before the role of mother in waiting. If you don't feel attractive it affects the overall sexual energy in the relationship. It's so easy for waiting couples to forget to do the fun stuff, to bury intimacy under timed intercourse and to forego romance in favor of fertility plans. Don't let that unfortunate scenario be your story. Childlessness doesn't often lead to divorce, it's the lack of intimacy and romance and the gradual transformation from lovers to strangers sharing a roof that leads to the divorce. Even if you are already stuck in a rut, you can put all your energies into saving your marriage and you would be surprised that the celebration of your reborn marriage may be marked with an unexpected bundle of joy. Sometimes we lose focus, but God never ever loses focus. Is your marriage healthy enough for a child to thrive emotionally and physically? If it isn't, a child won't fix it and it may be the very reason for the wait.

To thrive, you must make the best of your current situation in a manner that makes you happy, content and successful. One winning perspective is to focus your energies on your career, ministry, passion and the list of things you would not be able to do if you had children. I know a couple who built a successful company and moved from middle class to upper class in the ten years they waited for a child. What are you doing with the wait time? Are you saving up a nest egg? Or are you moping about feeling sorry for yourself and doing the barest minimum to get by? The wait time will not increase your income unless you are deliberate about it and if you are barely getting by now, what happens when you have children and your monthly expenses quadruple? You need to wake up and see the opportunities right under your nose, opportunities that would not exist or would be harder to accomplish when the children finally came. So, work on yourself while you wait. Work on the rough edges, your perceived weaknesses and on eliminating your emotional baggage so that when the wait does come to an end, you are whole, not broken and not scarred but the very best version of yourself ready to receive those blessings. While waiting, read about parenthood, read books and materials about qualities, attributes, qualifications and mindsets needed to accommodate the blessings you are waiting for. Success is when opportunity (what you are waiting for) meets preparation (what you need to be doing while waiting).

The waiting time is also an opportunity to thrive spiritually. Your spiritual health during this time is very important. Your relationship with the Lord will be the solid rock, enabling you to weather the storm of disappointment that comes with waiting to have children. Anna was always in the house of God. The bible says in Luke 2;36-37 that she lived with her husband only seven years before he died and doesn't mention if she had children, yet she lived a long life (she was 84) and was always worshipping night and day, fasting and praying. Seek His kingdom above all else. Put Him before your agendas, timelines, and priorities. Walk in faith and not fear. Walk in power, victory, and a sound mind. Do everything on time and in order because all your steps are ordered by Him, and you have good success. There's nothing stopping you from basking in His presence night and day. Every spare moment you have. It's an amazing way to occupy your heart, mind and time while you wait and there's never a soul who spends continual time in God's presence that doesn't reap unimaginable benefits. The bible says seek first the kingdom of God and His righteousness and all other things will be added unto you (Matthew 6:33). Don't miss the lesson to be learned. Waiting teaches us valuable lessons. Waiting may reveal toxic relationships in your life or strengths you didn't know you had or just show you how resilient or ingenious you can be. Don't look down on these life lessons. Encourage yourself with the testimonies of others who have walked in your shoes.

Don't let your wait make you feel less human. Everyone has someone or something they are waiting for, a meaningful relationship, a marriage, a job, a financial breakthrough, a business opportunity, freedom or just some good news. The list is endless. Because this is your lot in life doesn't mean you are worse off than the next person. It doesn't mean your situation cannot change in an instant. Your cross was made to fit your dimensions and situation, it is not heavier or lighter than the next person's cross despite how 'visible' it is. So, learn to block out negativity and avoid people and places that steal your joy because some people find out that focusing on the problems of others helps them momentarily forget theirs. Don't upset your balance because of someone else's negative coping mechanism. The bible says, because you look to Him you are radiant; your face will never be covered with shame (Psalm 34:5). Waiting gives us a unique story that can encourage someone else. You can't give good advice unless you have walked in a person's shoes. So, what better way to make waiting count than to encourage someone else who is waiting for the same reason, to keep going? A lot of people are not as strong as you are and encouraging someone else will give you an extra boost of positive energy.

Some days will be tough, but everyone knows some days there's going to be rain, that's why we all have umbrellas. Nobody goes looking to buy an umbrella when it is raining so you have to be prepared beforehand. Have a special playlist of all your favorite 'feel good' songs for the days your mood is a little low. Keep aside spa coupons or a little nest egg for some 'me time' pampering for the days when you feel less than stellar. Have a 'faith' playlist with your favorite worship songs and faith building sermons for days when you struggle with your faith. Have your favorite snack or food frozen in the freezer for a quick warm up in the microwave when you need some comfort food. Whatever you need should be within arm's reach because often times a bump in the road leaves no fore warning. And if the bad days keep rolling in without pause, you might want to consider a fresh start somewhere else- a new job, new house, new environment or new country, somewhere you can bask in the peace of an anonymous existence.

God says, "My thoughts for you are not thoughts of evil but thoughts of good to give you a future and hope" (Jeremiah 29:11). Yes, there will be times when it feels like the rains are pouring down real heavy and God seems so far away. Times when you want to crawl in a hole and weep far away from anyone and anything, when you just want to be left alone. So, what do you do then? You remember His promises. They bring comfort and assurance and hope for a better tomorrow. He says He will never leave you nor forsake you, His thoughts for you are not thoughts of evil but thoughts of good to give you a future and a hope. He makes everything work together for good for you. Those who trust in Him shall not be put to shame. Your expectations shall not be cut short. You will be a joyful mother of children. You will see your children's children. He will fill your mouth with laughter. He will give you peace that passes all understanding. Nothing is impossible for God. So, get out of bed, dress up and say 'thank you God because I know you have a plan' then wear your brightest smile. You are defying your circumstance and defying the devil and soon you will feel joy like a river envelope you like a cocoon and His peace seep through your every pore.

The bible says, eye hath not seen, nor ear heard, neither have entered into the heart of man, the things which God hath prepared for them that love him (1 Corinthians 2:9). Learn to say thank you even when you'd rather be saying 'No thank you' or 'Why Lord?' Develop an attitude of gratitude because He has prepared something amazing for you which is unfolding! Waiting makes the want or need more memorable and appreciated when it is finally in our grasp. It's so easy to take for granted the things we didn't wait or labor for. Don't waste your waiting time, it's the right time to do a lot of things. Life is a continuum, there are no pauses or vacuums. Abram kept moving, steadily making his way south, to the Negev (Genesis 12:9). He kept moving, he didn't know the end game, he wasn't sure of the final destination, but he kept moving. Don't ever stop! Make each day count so that when your expectations become a reality they won't be brought into an otherwise futile existence and if for reasons best known to God the wait lasts a lifetime, I want you to look back at that life and feel satisfied that it was a life well lived and thoroughly enjoyed!

Today, as I conclude a story that is far from over, I have many more things to be thankful for. I live in a new country with my husband, I have passed the exams I had to write barely 2 months after the ectopic pregnancy, and I am now a Specialist Physician. I did repeat fertility tests and both my fallopian tubes as well as the rest of my reproductive tract were intact and normal. I am a published author (well, I must be if you're reading this!). I am working on getting my sexy back- it's looking good so far, and I have travelled to many exciting countries and met so many interesting and amazing people-a couple of them who voluntarily chose never to have kids and shared their unique perspectives with me! I'm committed to living my best life while being a Jesus girl and I hope you can find the strength to do so too. I wouldn't have it any other way, my goal is simple- on the road less travelled, I will thrive!

Prayer

Dear Father, there's no way of knowing for sure how long I will wait or if the wait will come to an end but what I know for sure is that you are a faithful God, keeper of promises, lover of my soul. I am confident beyond doubt that your thoughts for me about this issue are of good and not evil, to give me a future and hope. Please help me Father to accept the future you have designed for me and not what I think the future should be, because your ways are infinitely higher than mine and so is your wisdom. Help me to trust you and to rest in your everlasting arms in Jesus' name. Amen

Action Points

1. Write a list of things you have learned about yourself and others since you started the wait.
2. Confess any jealousy or self-pity to the Lord.
3. Pray before going into a situation that could overwhelm you and ask God for strength and perspective and joy like a river.

…Sometimes the unexpected can be magical, life is what you make of it!

THE END!

Bible Verses About Conception, Pregnancy and Delivery

Our words are powerful. When you speak the word of God constantly into your situation it produces results. God says about His word, so is my word that goes out from my mouth: It will not return to me empty but will accomplish what I desire and achieve the purpose for which I sent it (Isaiah 55:11). David said, "I will worship toward thy holy temple, and praise thy name for thy loving-kindness and for thy truth: for thou hast magnified thy word above all thy name" (Psalm 138:2). God honors His word above His name. God is not human, that he should lie, not a human being, that he should change his mind. Does he speak and then not act? Does he promise and not fulfill? (Numbers 23:19). So, speak His words over and over on the days you feel like and the days you don't and watch it boost your faith and change your situation!

Conception

- *Deuteronomy 7:14* - I will be blessed more than any other people; neither my husband nor I nor any of our household will be childless, nor will any of our livestock be without young.
- *Psalm 34:5* - Because I look to Him, I am radiant; my face will never be covered with shame.
- *Hebrews 6:10* - God is not unjust; he will not forget my work and the love I have shown him as I have helped his people and continue to help them.

- *Hebrews 6:11* - I will show this same diligence to the very end, so that what I hope for may be fully realized.
- *Hebrews 6:14* - "He will surely bless me and give me many descendants."
- *Hebrews 10:23* - I will hold unswervingly to the hope I profess, for He who promised is faithful.
- *Hebrews 11:11* - And by faith even Sarah, who was past childbearing age, was enabled to bear children because she considered him faithful who had made the promise.

1 John 5:14

- *Isaiah 29:17* - Soon—and it will not be very long— the forests of Lebanon will become a fertile field, and the fertile field will yield bountiful crops.
- *Psalms 113:9* - He honors the childless wife in her home; he makes her happy by giving her children. Praise the LORD!
- *Luke 1:45* - Blessed is she who has believed that the Lord would fulfill his promises to her!
- *Psalm 34:4* - I sought the Lord, and he answered me; he delivered me from all my fears.
- *Psalm 23:1* - The Lord is my shepherd, I lack nothing.
- *Job 8:21* - He will yet fill your mouth with laughter and your lips with shouts of joy.
- *Isaiah 49:15* - "Can a mother forget the baby at her breast and have no compassion on the child she has borne? Though she may forget, I will not forget you!
- *Psalm 128:3* - Your wife shall be like a fruitful vine in the very heart of your house, your children like olive plants all around your table.
- *Psalm 127: 3-5* - Children are indeed a heritage from the LORD, and the fruit of the womb is His reward. Like arrows in the hand of a warrior, so are children born in one's youth. Blessed is the man whose quiver is full of them.
- *Luke 1:37* - For no word from God will ever fail.

Pregnancy

- *Exodus 23:26* - None shall be barren or miscarry in your land. The number of your days, I will fulfil.
- *Jeremiah 1:5* - Before I formed you in the womb, I knew you and before you were delivered out of the womb, I sanctified you.
- *Psalm 139:13* - God has possessed your reins (He controls everything that will happen to you from conception to delivery) and He has covered you in the womb.
- *Psalm 71:6* - From birth you have relied on Him; He brought you forth from your mother's womb. You will ever praise Him.
- *Psalm 4:8* - I lie down and sleep in peace
- *Psalms 91* - I am well and whole for my God watches over me.
- *Colossians 1:16* - my children were created in Him, through him and for him.
- *Colossians 1:17* - In Him my children are held together, firmly implanted in my womb.
- *Colossians 2:19* - God causes my babies to grow due to their connection to Christ.
- *Colossians 3:3* - My babies' lives are hidden with Christ in God.
- *Colossians 3:12* - My babies are clothed with compassion, kindness, humility, gentleness and patience.
- *Colossians 3:20* - My babies will be obedient to their father and me all their lives in Jesus' name.
- *John 10:29* - My Father, who has given my babies to me, is greater than all; no one can snatch them out of my Father's hand.
- *2 Corinthians 12:9* - But he said to me, "My grace is sufficient for you.
- *2 Timothy 1:12* - I know whom I have believed and am convinced that He is able to guard the babies I have entrusted to him until that day.
- *2 Timothy 1:14* - I will guard the good deposit that was entrusted to me— my babies. I will guard them with the help of the Holy Spirit who lives in me.

- *Malachi 3:11* - And I will rebuke the devourer for your sakes, and he shall not destroy the fruits of your ground; neither shall your vine cast her fruit before the time in the field, saith the Lord of hosts.
- *Psalms 89:34* - No, I will not break my covenant; I will not take back a single word I said.

Delivery

- *Isaiah 66:9* - The Lord is the one who makes birth possible. And he will see that Zion has many more children. The Lord has spoken.
- *2 Timothy 4:18* - The Lord will rescue me from every evil attack and will bring me safely to his heavenly kingdom. To him be glory for ever and ever. Amen
- *Hebrews 2:13* - And again, "I will put my trust in him." Here am I, and the children God has given me."
- *Hebrews 2:14* - Since the children have flesh and blood, Jesus too shared in their humanity so that by his death he might break the power of him who holds the power of death—that is, the devil.
- *Hebrews 4:16* - I will approach God's throne of grace with confidence, so that I may receive mercy and find grace to help me in my time of need.
- *Hebrews 13:5* - "Never will He leave me; never will He forsake me."
- *1 Peter 5:7* - I cast all my anxiety on him because he cares for me.
- *Luke 1:14* - My babies will be a joy and delight to me, and many will rejoice because of their birth.
- *Proverbs 23:18* - For surely there is an end; and my expectation shall not be cut off.
- *Job 22:28* - What you decide on will be done, and light will shine on your ways.
- *Isaiah 29:23* - For when they see their many children and all the blessings, I have given them, they will recognize the holiness of the Holy One of Jacob. They will stand in awe of the God of Israel.
- *Philippians 1:6* - Being confident of this, that he who began a good work in me will carry this pregnancy and my babies on to completion until the day of Christ Jesus.

Infertility and Fertility Testing

Infertility is defined as not being able to get pregnant despite having frequent, unprotected sex, at least three to four times a week for at least a year. This is also called Primary Infertility. Secondary infertility is the inability to conceive or carry a baby to term after previously giving birth to a baby. It's advisable to go see a doctor after one year of actively trying for a baby so you can get checked out and guided. However, if you are fast approaching 35 or your husband is fast approaching 40, seeing a doctor after trying for 6 months is advisable because of the observed decline in fertility for women after the age of 35 and men after the age of 40.

Studies have shown that about 40% of infertility cases are due to male factors, about 40% are due to female factors, and the remaining 20% are either a combination of both partners' factors or are unknown/unexplained. You and your husband need to be on the same page so that you both do the tests together. Assumptions about the cause of infertility prior to testing often lead to guilt, disharmony and sometimes overconfidence which may delay diagnosis and treatment.

Fertility and Reproductive health tests for Women

1. Ultrasound scan- to check your womb and ovaries (pelvic and transvaginal ultrasound scan)
2. Hormone assays- Estrogen, Progesterone, Prolactin, Thyroid Function tests, Estradiol, Dehydroepiandrosterone Sulfate, Follicle

Stimulating Hormone, Luteinizing Hormone, Testosterone-hormones that influence fertility

3. Endocervical swab, High vaginal swab- to check for infections like Chlamydia
4. Pap Smear- to screen for cervical cancer
5. Anti-Mullerian Hormone- to check your egg supply (ovarian reserve)
6 Follicular tracking or Folliculometry- to monitor ovulation (see below)
7. Hysterosalpingogram- to test the patency of your fallopian tubes

Fertility and Reproductive health tests for Men

1. Seminal fluid analysis- check for defects in the number, shape and movement of sperm
2. Hormone assays- Free and total testosterone, Luteinizing hormone, Follicle Stimulating hormone, Prolactin and Sex hormone binding globulin- hormones that influence fertility
3. Testicular ultrasound scan- to check for the structural patency of the testes and scrotum
4. Urine test- to screen for infections like Chlamydia

Ovulation is the period when your egg is released every month. If you have doubts about when you ovulate, here are some options to help (if your period is regular):

1. Speak to a health worker to help calculate your ovulation days.
2. Download a period tracker application which will track your ovulation for you
3. Buy a 60 pack of ovulation strips and pee on it every morning for 2 months starting from the first day of your menstrual period so you can compare two cycles and deduce when you ovulate.

4. Keep a record of your daily basal body temperature using a digital thermometer- your basal body temperature is your body's lowest temperature at rest and is usually measured as soon as you wake up and before any physical activity. It rises by about 0.4 degrees Celsius just after ovulation due to Progesterone hormone which is secreted when an egg is released. The basal body temperature returns back to normal if a pregnancy doesn't occur, just before menstruation.

5. Cervical mucus secretion- just before ovulation, the hormone Estrogen causes the cervical mucus to be like egg white- stretchy, viscous and thin. This helps sperm reach the egg. After ovulation, Progesterone makes the cervical mucus thick and sticky. Aim to have unprotected sex when the cervical mucus is like egg white consistency.

6. Follicular tracking or Folliculometry- Series of ultrasound scans to determine how follicles are growing in the ovaries and when one of them ruptures to release an egg.

If your period isn't regular, you may require the help of a gynecologist to track your ovulation.

Assisted Conception Options

Assisted conception or assisted reproduction technology is the use of medical procedures and fertility medication to help a couple conceive by removing eggs from the woman's body or a female donor's body and then mixing them with sperm from the man's body or a male donor's body to make embryos which are returned to the woman's womb or a surrogate's womb. There are different types available, and you and your doctor would decide which is best for you if required.

In vitro fertilization (IVF) is the technique of letting fertilization of the male and female gametes (sperm and egg) occur outside the female body. There are many techniques usually used in in vitro fertilization including:

1. Transvaginal ovum retrieval (OVR) simply referred to as egg retrieval, is the process whereby a small needle is inserted through the back of the vagina and guided via ultrasound into the ovarian follicles to collect the fluid that contains the eggs. Embryo transfer is the step in the process whereby one or several embryos are placed into the uterus of the female with the intent to establish a pregnancy.

2. Assisted zona hatching (AZH) is performed shortly before the embryo is transferred to the uterus. A small opening is made in the outer layer surrounding the egg in order to help the embryo hatch out and aid in the implantation process of the growing embryo.

3. Intracytoplasmic sperm injection (ICSI). This is beneficial in the case of male factor infertility where sperm counts are very low or failed fertilization occurred with previous IVF attempt(s). The ICSI

procedure involves a single sperm carefully injected into the center of an egg using a microneedle. With ICSI, only one sperm per egg is needed. Without ICSI, you need between 50,000 and 100,000. This method is also sometimes employed when donor sperm is used.

4. Autologous endometrial coculture is a possible treatment for patients who have failed previous IVF attempts or who have poor embryo quality. The patient's fertilized eggs are placed on top of a layer of cells from the patient's own womb lining, creating a more natural environment for embryo development.

5. In zygote intrafallopian transfer (ZIFT), egg cells are removed from the woman's ovaries and fertilized in the laboratory; the resulting zygote is then placed into the fallopian tube (an embryo develops from a zygote).

6. Cytoplasmic transfer is the technique in which the contents of a fertile egg from a donor are injected into the infertile egg of the patient along with the sperm.

7. Preimplantation genetic diagnosis (PGD) involves the use of genetic screening mechanisms such as fluorescent in-situ hybridization (FISH) or comparative genomic hybridization (CGH) to help identify genetically abnormal embryos and improve health outcomes. It is also used for gender selection.

8. Embryo splitting can be used for twinning to increase the number of available embryos.

9. Mitochondrial replacement therapy (MRT, sometimes called mitochondrial donation) is a special form of IVF in which some or all of the future baby's mitochondrial DNA comes from a third party. This technique is used in cases when mothers carry genes for mitochondrial diseases.

10. In gamete intrafallopian transfer (GIFT) a mixture of sperm and eggs is placed directly into a woman's fallopian tubes using laparoscopy following a transvaginal ovum retrieval.

11. Reproductive surgery- for treatment e.g., fallopian tube obstruction and vas deferens obstruction, or reversing a vasectomy by a reverse vasectomy or for retrieval- in surgical sperm retrieval (SSR), sperm is obtained from the vas deferens, epididymis or directly from the testis.

12. By cryopreservation, eggs, sperm, embryos and reproductive tissue can be preserved for later IVF.

13 Surrogacy is a legal arrangement whereby a woman (the surrogate mother) agrees to become pregnant and give birth to a child for a couple who are (their egg and/or sperm have been used) or will become (a donor was used) the parents of the child and hands relinquishes her rights to the child as soon as the child is born. A woman may seek a surrogacy arrangement when pregnancy is medically impossible or when pregnancy risks are too dangerous for the intended mother. The surrogate may be the biological mother if her eggs were used or just the birth mother if all she did was carry the pregnancy to term.

References:

1. Zegers-Hochschild, F; for the International Committee for Monitoring Assisted Reproductive Technology and the World Health Organization; et al. (November 2009). "International Committee for Monitoring Assisted Reproductive Technology (ICMART) and the World Health Organization (WHO) revised glossary of ART terminology, 2009" (PDF). Fertility and Sterility. 92 (5): 1520–4.

2. Bhatia, Kalsang; Martindale, Elizabeth A.; Rustamov, Oybek; Nysenbaum, Anthony M. (2009). "Surrogate pregnancy: an essential guide for clinicians". The Obstetrician & Gynecologist. 11 (1): 49–54.

Printed in Great Britain
by Amazon

80719804R00071